In Days Gone By

WORLD FOLKLORE SERIES

1991. *Folk Stories of the Hmong: Peoples of Laos, Thailand, and Vietnam.* By Norma J. Livo and Dia Cha.

1992. *Images of a People: Tlingit Myths and Legends.* By Mary Helen Pelton and Jacqueline DiGennaro.

1994. *Hyena and the Moon: Stories to Tell from Kenya.* By Heather McNeil.

1994. *The Corn Woman: Stories and Legends of the Hispanic Southwest.* By Angel Vigil.

1994. *Thai Tales: Folktales of Thailand.* Retold by Supaporn Vathanaprida. Edited by Margaret Read MacDonald.

1996. *In Days Gone By: Folklore and Traditions of the Pennsylvania Dutch.* By Audrey Burie Kirchner and Margaret R. Tassia.

Selections Available on Audiocassette

1995. *Hyena and the Moon: Stories to Listen to from Kenya.* By Heather McNeil.

1995. *The Corn Woman: Audio Stories and Legends of the Hispanic Southwest.* English and Spanish versions. By Angel Vigil. Spanish version read by Juan Francisco Marín.

In Days Gone By

Folklore and Traditions
of the Pennsylvania Dutch

Audrey Burie Kirchner
and
Margaret R. Tassia

Line Drawings by Erin Kirk

1996
Libraries Unlimited, Inc.
Englewood, Colorado

Libraries Unlimited, Inc.
P.O. Box 6633
Englewood, CO 80155-6633
(800) 237-6124

Production Editor: Kevin W. Perizzolo
Copy Editor: Jason Cook
Typesetting and Interior Design: Judy Gay Matthews

Library of Congress Cataloging-in-Publication Data

Kirchner, Audrey Burie, 1937-
   In days gone by : folklore and traditions of the Pennsylvania
Dutch / Audrey Burie Kirchner and Margaret R. Tassia ; line drawings
by Erin Kirk.
   xiv, 132 p.   19x26 cm.
   Includes bibliographical references.
   ISBN 1-56308-381-7
   1. Pennsylvania Dutch--Folklore.   2. Pennsylvania Dutch.
3. Folklore--Pennsylvania.   I. Title.   II. Series.
GR111.G47K57   1996
398'.089310748--dc20   95-48860
                                                        CIP

Dedication

To the memory of my beloved cousin, Capt. James R. Burie (USMC), with whom I shared so many wonderful moments growing up on "Cabbage Hill"; and to his loving family, who carry on his legacy.

To Stephen and Katie, who captivate my heart.

And to Leo, always Leo.

—A.B.K.

To the memory of Peter A. Tassia and Christine R. (Ganse) Tassia, who taught all of their children to appreciate an individual's culture and heritage.

—M.R.T.

Contents

Part II
Folklore

Chapter 11—Plant Legends 55

Chapter 12—Tall Tales 59

Chapter 13—Folktales 63

Part III
Recipes

Part IV
Story Sources and
Selected Bibliography

Acknowledgments

The authors are indebted to those who so willingly gave of their expertise, advice, and resources to make this book a reality. We give our deepest appreciation to the following:

Erin Kirk, art teacher, Penn Manor School District, Manor Township, Lancaster County, Pennsylvania, for her ability to capture and portray, in her line drawings, the essence of the themes and motifs that dominate Pennsylvania German folk art and folklife. Her enthusiasm and commitment are essential to the spirit of this book.

Catherine Burie Kiss, who so painstakingly typed the manuscript and prepared the diskette files. She persevered through revisions, additions, and corrections, and willingly took time to do an excellent job. She provided us with her expertise while also being the busy mother of two children and a part of the work force outside the home.

Dr. C. Richard Beam, German Professor Emeritus, Millersville University of Pennsylvania, Millersville, Pennsylvania, who honored us with his time and guidance. Dr. Beam, a nationally known authority on Pennsylvania folklife and folklore, gained prominence for his diligent work in compiling a Pennsylvania German dialect dictionary. He is respected by all groups of Pennsylvania Germans for his love of the culture.

Carol E. Faill, Director, Leonard and Mildred Rothman Gallery, Franklin and Marshall College, Lancaster, Pennsylvania, who graciously shared her knowledge of Pennsylvania folk art and provided excellent photographic examples of Pennsylvania German artifacts. She has a keen interest in helping children discover the uniqueness of a culture. The Rothman Gallery, a must for people visiting the area, houses an outstanding collection of Pennsylvania German folk art and realia preserved by Franklin and Marshall College.

Elizabeth Johnson, Educational Director, Landis Valley Museum, Lancaster County, Pennsylvania, who provided photos and information concerning the daily lives of the Pennsylvania Germans. Her efforts have helped produce a museum that is an entrance into the folklife of the early Pennsylvania Germans for the many children and adults who visit.

Henry J. Kauffman, Professor Emeritus, Millersville University of Pennsylvania, Millersville, Pennsylvania, who gave of his time, talent, and expertise to provide us with information about the daily lives of the Pennsylvania Germans. Attesting to his knowledge and love of the culture are many books and articles, as well as his collection of Pennsylvania German artifacts in the Henry J. Kauffman Museum at Rockford (historical home of General Edward Hand), Lancaster County, Pennsylvania.

Arthur L. Reist, retired teacher, Conestoga Valley School District, Lancaster County, Pennsylvania, a noted authority on the Conestoga wagon and the farm life of the Pennsylvania Germans, and an expert on the Conestoga wagoner's life. He has written articles and books on many aspects of folklife, and he is in constant demand to explicate and demonstrate the farming techniques associated with the Pennsylvania Germans.

Dorothy Frey and Grace Miller, long-time Pennsylvania German storytellers who read the manuscript and offered constructive suggestions for telling the stories and for locating sources and collections. They also gave us a taste of the dialect. Being of Pennsylvania German background, they have "lived" this culture—and kept it alive with their storytelling.

Millersville University of Pennsylvania, Millersville, Pennsylvania, for preserving books, periodicals, and materials in their archives. Robert Coley and Dorothea Zimmerman deserve special thanks for their patience and for giving us access to the university's collection.

Franklin and Marshall College, Lancaster, Pennsylvania, for preserving the materials donated or purchased for their permanent collection. Of note, Franklin and Marshall College initiated a "Pennsylvania German Studies Program" (the first of its kind); many of the authors we consulted taught courses in this program, which endeavored to preserve the folklife and the folklore of the Pennsylvania Germans.

George F. Martin and E. J. Martin, who solidified our conviction that what we learn as a child about our heritage and culture stays with us for a lifetime. Their quest for the "Schnitzelbank" song chart, which they recalled from childhood and which George wishes to share with children, will be another important step in preserving the culture of a very special people, the Pennsylvania Germans.

Introduction

A unique culture exists today in the lives of the Pennsylvania Germans, also known as the Pennsylvania Dutch. This culture's presence in the United States begins with the arrival of German-speaking immigrants in the colony of Pennsylvania between 1683 and 1783. They presented in themselves a unique cross-section of people: several religious groups, unaffiliated individuals, farm people, craft people, construction workers, and university graduates. The name Pennsylvania Dutch was given to these German-speaking immigrants by English-speaking people in America who mispronounced the German word *Deutsch*, meaning "folk" or "German."

The beliefs and customs of the Pennsylvania German culture have endured to this day. Some Pennsylvania German groups have assimilated beliefs and customs of other cultures; still, many groups remain uninfluenced, retaining the traditions inherent to their individual backgrounds. It is of value to note that the Pennsylvania German traditions have spread far beyond the borders of Pennsylvania.

The purpose of this book is to present the fascinating folklife and folklore of the Pennsylvania Germans not only to teachers and students but to anyone interested in exploring a culture that continues to influence our lives—and more visibly so today, as Pennsylvania Germans settle throughout the United States. We hope that this book will provide a meaningful resource, especially in light of the fact that much of this folklore is not readily available to the general public. The authors feel that it is vital to disseminate the rich folklife and folklore of the Pennsylvania Germans so that it will not become lost, relegated to the shelves of historical archives. In some of the folk stories collected here, readers will find a similarity to themes and plots of folk stories from other European cultures, which indicates that not only did the Pennsylvania German people assimilate values from their neighboring cultural groups in Pennsylvania, but they also assimilated values of their neighboring cultural groups in Europe.

Storytelling continues to be a favorite pastime of the Pennsylvania Germans. The reader should remember, however, that although the Amish (one of the groups that makes up the Pennsylvania German culture) are great storytellers and although storytelling is a favorite activity of the Amish, their stories are rooted in everyday happenings or religion. The Amish shun tales that tell of magic or make-believe.

Part I provides a history of the Pennsylvania Germans, including information related to areas such as the Pennsylvania Dutch dialect, family and home life, folk art, holidays, beliefs, superstitions, and contributions. We have made every effort to authenticate the information and to preserve the dignity of the various German-speaking groups that bonded to become the Pennsylvania Germans.

In Part II, we present a tapestry of folklore. The stories reflect important components of Pennsylvania German life, traditions, beliefs, and superstitions. Included are childhood rhymes, tall tales, plant legends, and folktales. The folktales represent a variety of stories, such as tales of long ago, brauche and hexe stories, spirit stories, stories of special days, and stories about a cunning fellow named Eileschpiggel. We have made every effort to preserve the original intent and flavor of the stories collected here, balancing this attempt with our endeavor to preserve the oral tradition. We have culled much of the folklore from the original sources, including original translations from the Pennsylvania Dutch dialect. We hope that you, too, will come to treasure the folklife and folklore of the Pennsylvania Germans, a very vital presence in our cultural history.

Audrey Burie Kirchner
Margaret R. Tassia

Part I

Folklife

Chapter 1

The Pennsylvania Germans

A History

The history of the Pennsylvania Germans is a fascinating and informative portrait of an enduring culture that helped to establish the United States of America as an independent country. The founding of Germantown in 1683 marked the first permanent Pennsylvania German settlement in America. By 1790, the Pennsylvania Germans represented at least one-third of the population. Most of these German-speaking people (or "folk") had a great belief in the goodness and mercy of God, and hoped that their life in America held great promise. Regardless of personal beliefs, through years of working and living together, they formed a unique ethnic group. The people had in common such traits as love of family, church, and community; a language that not only enveloped German but was developing into a unique dialect of its own; and the ethic of hard work.

This group popularly known as the "Pennsylvania Dutch" must give credit for their resulting identity to an Englishman by the name of William Penn. Charles II, King of England, gave young Penn (who was heir to the estate of his father, Admiral William Penn) a parcel of land in the new world in lieu of payment for a debt of eighty pounds of sterling owed to his father by the royal family.

The younger William Penn espoused the Quaker philosophy and yearned to establish a haven for Europeans who had been suffering because of their religious beliefs. His quest became known in history as "Penn's Holy Experiment." The haven was to become, ultimately, the state of Pennsylvania. Penn was also aware that, in addition to providing a home for religious freedom, "Penn's Woods" had to be a financial success. This meant taming and converting wilderness into farms and towns; and he set out to interest people in becoming colonists in his land.

During the seventeenth century, two centuries after the Reformation, much of central Europe was still in political and religious turmoil. This was the era of the Reformation aftermath—people severed their ties with the Roman Catholic Church and began following the popular teachings of John Hus, Martin Luther, George Fox, John Calvin, Menno Simons, and others,—establishing new formal religious groups, such as the Lutheran and German Reformed Church. In addition, there were those who opposed and distrusted formal

religious practices. Reacting to the formalism and intellectualism that had occurred, a religious movement stressing Bible study and personal religious experiences gained followers. This movement was known as Pietism, and its followers were known as Pietists.

Politically, Germany embodied a loose confederation of principalities, duchies, and kingdoms whose common bond was the German language. An area that had been a particular scene of great upheaval was the area of Germany around the Rhine river, known as "The Palatine." Here, the people fought wars to gain religious freedom—but lost the right to worship according to one's conscience. Significant numbers of people grasping for religious freedom fled to Holland and Switzerland, which border the Rhine and The Palatine.

It was to The Palatine that William Penn traveled to recruit settlers. While staying in Frankfurt, he set up The Frankfurt Land Company to sell or finance the purchase of land to arouse interest in "Penn's Woods." People who were unable to pay for the land sold themselves as indentured servants to families before departure and worked for those individuals until they had satisfied their loans. Sometimes, people indentured themselves to the ship's captain, who, in turn, sold them in America.

These original immigrants, who would become the Pennsylvania Germans, came from parts of Scandinavia, Switzerland, Holland, and The Palatine. This included Alsace, Lorraine, Bavaria, Luxembourg, Prussia, Selesia (a former province partly in Prussia and Poland), Moravia (a former province in central Czechoslovakia), and Saxony. Among the religious sects represented during the colony's first 20 years in America were Swiss Mennonites, Dutch Quakers, Frankfurt Pietists, Selesian Schwenkfelders, Saxon Herrhuters, Danish Doompellars, Palatine Reformed, Wurttemberg Lutherans, and Alsatian Huguenots. The Amish, the Dunkards (Church of the Brethren), and the Moravians formed another large number of immigrants during the 1700s. Still another group of immigrants were the soldiers (from a part of Germany called Hesse) hired by England to fight against the colonists in America during the Revolutionary War. Many of these soldiers were taken prisoner in Pennsylvania. While serving time in prison, they became friendly with other German-speaking people. When freed after the war, many Hessian soldiers decided to stay in Pennsylvania and make it their home. Tied together by hope and a desire to be forever free from oppression, these peoples settled and established homes, farms, and towns in eastern Pennsylvania.

The very first settlement was Germantown, which was two-hours walking distance from Philadelphia. Francis Daniel Schaffer, who latinized his last name to read "Pastorius," bought land from William Penn for himself and for people from the town of Crefeld (Krefeld, located near the Rhine). These people, known as "The Crefelders" (Krefelders), were mostly Lowland Dutch Quakers and German Mennonites. It is of historical significance to note that these German-speaking Pietists led by Pastorius were the first to speak out against black slavery. Perhaps this anti-slavery stand was a reaction to the plight of many Mennonites who had been sold to someone for seven years as payment for their voyage to Philadelphia. If parents died on the trip, their children were sold and obliged to work for the "owners" until they were twenty-one years of age. When set free, a man was given a horse and a suit of clothes. A woman was given clothes and a cow. Once on their own, the men and women were free to work for themselves.

As time went by, new German-speaking settlers made their homes well beyond the borders of Germantown. Today, the Pennsylvania Germans are recognized as "The Plain People" and "The Church People." The descendants of both groups have kept alive the traditional and cultural heritages of their people (or "folk").

The Plain People comprised the many orders of Amish, Mennonites, Church of the Brethren, and Schwenkfelders. These people rejected worldly ways of dress and home life to maintain a simple dress and lifestyle reminiscent of Europe before the modern era. Several groups have retained their early beliefs in all ways, while others have assimilated modern dress and certain modern conveniences. Their contribution to what has become the Pennsylvania Dutch culture is the handing down of customs and beliefs held over many centuries.

The Church People are those people of the Lutheran and Reformed religions, Quakers and Moravians. They have, for the most part, assimilated the dress and lifestyles of the modern day. This group has preserved the folk art, folklore, and holiday customs of their past. The paragraphs that follow briefly introduce the reader to specific information concerning several of the groups who contributed (and still contribute) to the vitality of Pennsylvania German folklife and folklore.

The Plain People

The Mennonites

The Mennonites are followers of Menno Simons, from whom they took their name. Menno Simons's followers included many German-speaking Anabaptists in Germany, Holland, and Switzerland during the 1530s. In the early days, people considered the Anabaptists to be a radical group. They believed that "church" was a gathering of people united by faith, repentance, obedience, and discipline. Therefore, the Anabaptists espoused the belief that baptism as an entrance to the community should be given only to believers old enough to voluntarily choose group membership and the renouncement of sin. Anabaptists sought daily to "prove" their goodness. They were nicknamed Anabaptists (rebaptizers) because adults who had been baptized as children were rebaptized as adults. They continued to condemn government interference and government involvement in religion and were persecuted by Roman Catholics and other Protestant movements.

The first Mennonites belonged to a church organized in Zurich, Switzerland. They called themselves "Swiss Brethren" or "Swiss Mennonites." Many settled in southern Germany, France, and—eventually—in Pennsylvania. Today, several branches of Mennonites exist. Mennonites prefer plain ways of dressing, living, and worshipping. Mennonites base their beliefs on the Bible, particularly "The Sermon on the Mount" from the

Jacob H. Landis (1908-1977) with calf at the Amos R. Landis homestead, East Lampeter Township, Lancaster County, Pennsylvania in 1918. (Courtesy of Carol E. Leaman)

New Testament. They believe that this sermon forbids going to war, swearing oaths, or holding offices that rely on the use of force. Today, the Mennonites are a thriving community. They are farmers, business people, doctors, teachers, builders, and artisans. The community is well known for its efforts to help those in need, both in this country and around the world, through missionary work.

The Amish

In the 1690s, a Protestant group broke away from the Swiss Mennonites in Switzerland and became known as "The Old Order Amish." They were named after Jacob Ammon, who led them away from the Mennonite faith because of disagreements over discipline. Ammon, a Mennonite preacher in Bern, Switzerland, began to strictly enforce the doctrine of Meidung (shunning, which is the practice of completely avoiding someone) to punish a member who had been unfaithful to the sect. The Mennonites felt that this punishment was too severe.

Over time, the Amish built their unique culture, which stressed separation from the world. Their beliefs forbid them to go to war, take oaths, or hold public office. Their personal lifestyles reflect basic simplicity. The Amish desire to stay apart from the world in their daily life and dress. Their Ordnung (rules) also ban using electricity, and owning telephones and automobiles. Horse-drawn wagons and buggies are their mode of transportation. However, Amish may ride in a car, bus, or train if not for pleasure. All this is part of their desire to stay apart from the world.

Members of the sect meet every two weeks for worship in someone's home. Services can be as long as three hours and preachers are chosen by lot. Members sing "a cappella" because musical instruments are forbidden at church services and in the home. The Ausbund (hymnal) used during worship is the oldest Protestant hymnal. It was first printed in 1564 and contains 140 hymns that reflect an influence of the Gregorian chants of the early monks. These chants describe the sufferings of the martyrs and their heroism for God.

Education is limited to the eighth grade. Although most Amish men are farmers, building and carpentry are also prevalent occupations. Amish women traditionally take care of the home and gardens and help sell produce. The people have simple tastes in entertainment. Activities include Sunday night "singings," buggy races, barn raisings, quilting parties, weddings, and a few holiday celebrations.

Today, most descendants of the Pennsylvania Germans have adapted to modern dress. However, the Old Order Amish culture has kept to the "old ways." The Amish dress is a curiosity to "The English," the Amish name for those outside their sect. The Amish men and boys wear black trousers, vests, and coats. The coats have no lapels or outside pockets. During winter, Amish men wear a low-crowned, broad-brimmed black felt hat. During summer, they wear the same style of hat, but one made of straw. Also during winter, the men wear an overcoat with a short cape. The mens' and boys' shirts and the womens' and girls' dresses are made from brighter colors of blue, purple, red, and green.

The women and girls wear black bonnets, black aprons, and black winter shawls. Women also wear white prayer caps, as do most women of the plain sects, because of a biblical injunction that warns that it is vain not to cover one's hair. Buttons are never used on Amish clothing. This is a reaction to the military buttons of the soldiers who persecuted their ancestors. Military disdain is also the reason that Amish men never grow a mustache (because it was popular with soldiers). However, the men grow a beard once they have married.

It is believed that the first Amish arrived in Pennsylvania by 1737. The oldest settlement is in Lancaster County, Pennsylvania. Today other large communities are found in Ohio, Indiana, Iowa, Illinois, and Florida.

In the twentieth century, some Old Order Amish wished to modernize their lifestyle more than the bishops would allow. A new sect emerged—the Church Amish (or Beachey Amish). They were called Church Amish because they built meeting houses for worship, or Beachey Amish after their founder, Moses Beachey. The members of this sect have become more modern in their dress and are permitted to drive automobiles and tractors. They may also use electricity.

The Church of the Brethren

The Church of the Brethren was first established in 1708 by Alexander Mack, who lived in the town of Schresheim in The Palatine. The group suffered persecution in Germany, but reorganized themselves after twenty families from the sect arrived in Germantown, Pennsylvania in 1719. The first congregation worshipped together at Christmas in 1723. Finally, in 1729, Mack arrived in

America with a large group of followers, and the Church of the Brethren became a thriving community. Most settled in Lancaster County, Pennsylvania.

Two basic practices of this group that led them from the Reformed Church were baptism by trine immersion (the word *trine* means "triple") and foot-washing, which were not condoned by the Reformed Church. At one time, the sect was known as "Dunkards" or "Dunkers," from the Pennsylvania German word *dunke*, meaning "to immerse." Baptisms were usually conducted in a flowing stream.

The Brethren believed in nonresistance. To this day, they teach "alternative" service in place of military service. However, a man may follow his conscience and become a member of the armed services if he so chooses. The Brethren lifestyle calls for simple living and dress. Members met for worship in plain meeting houses. One tradition that has gained recognition is the "Love Feast," which includes hymn singing, testimony to the power and love of God, foot-washing, communion, hand shaking, and "the holy kiss of charity" on the cheek. A supper and fellowship follow the feast.

Today, the Brethren are less plain in dress. They continue to be active in missionary work throughout the world. Their belief in quality education has led to the establishment of six colleges and a seminary.

The Schwenkfelders

This religious group, formed in Selesia, followed the teachings of Casper Schwenkfeld von Ossig, an Anabaptist who was a religious reformer in Germany during the 1500s. Schwenkfelders disagreed with Luther's emphasis on the Bible and believed that, in addition to needing the Bible, people needed the living word (or "spirit of Christ in man").

The group suffered religious persecution in Selesia and fled. Between 1731 and 1737, the entire group of Schwenkfelders emigrated to Pennsylvania searching for religious freedom. Most settled into farming in southeast Pennsylvania near Philadelphia.

Today, with approximately 3,000 members, the Schwenkfelders still base their religious faith on the spiritual life of the individual. Worship services are simple. Schwenkfelders promote Bible study, education, and a conservative lifestyle. However, they have abandoned the plain clothing and other characteristics that set them apart from "The Church People." This sect, too, is especially active in the mission fields.

The Church People

The Lutheran Church

Martin Luther, a professor at the University of Wittenberg, was a leader of the Reformation. He translated the Bible into German, and many give him credit for refining and promoting the German language. Luther pondered the question of how an individual could find favor with God. He concluded that it was a gift from God, and that God's grace and mercy would purify the sins of mankind. Luther believed that each person has direct access to God. He preached that the Bible was

the final authority and the basis for church teaching. Followers of Luther willingly accepted an established state church; the idea of bearing arms for the government, if necessary; and the actual presence of Christ's body and blood in the bread and wine of the communion service (transubstantiation).

Lutherans were spared the religious persecution that many other denominations suffered. It was the desire to relocate, for economic reasons, that caused many German-speaking people of the Lutheran faith to emigrate to Pennsylvania. According to record, the first "coming together" of a German Lutheran group in Pennsylvania occurred in 1717.

The Reformed Church

Ulrich Zwingli, born the same year as Martin Luther, is credited as the founder of the Reformed Church. The Reformed Church, called "The Mother of Sects," has widely influenced other church movements with few remaining uninfluenced by its views. These views included beliefs that

the bread and wine of the communion service are merely symbols, that laymen share authority with clergy, that a free church should exist in a free state, and that clergy should be educated and treated with honor.

In The Palatine, members of the Reformed Church were not allowed to practice their religion with the freedom they desired. For example, the members were forced to share church buildings with Lutherans and Catholics and were not permitted to use their own "Heidelberg Catechism." The University of Heidelberg was a stronghold of the Reformed Church. When Jesuits joined the faculty, members of the Reformed Church left by the thousands for Pennsylvania. This emigration helped make Pennsylvania a Protestant colony and The Palatine primarily Roman Catholic. The first recorded information about the members of the Reformed Church in Pennsylvania indicates that they arrived in 1725. By 1730, the members of the Reformed Church accounted for more than half of the Pennsylvania German population, outnumbered only by the Lutherans in the latter half of the century.

The Quakers

Lowland Dutch Quakers were among the first settlers in Germantown, Pennsylvania. George Fox, who developed "The Religious Society of Friends" in England, founded the Quaker religion. Fox preached that the "inner light" of Christ dwells in the hearts of ordinary people. His reforms, based upon the belief that all life is sacramental, spread to central Europe and are alive today throughout the world. Basic principles include a trust in the Holy Spirit, faith that all people are able to receive the Spirit, and reliance on inward spiritual experiences. Those who followed this religion considered themselves to be truly spiritual and living according to God's will. The name "Quaker" was coined during the time of religious oppression. It was an insult leveled by a judge whom Fox had told to "tremble at the Word of the Lord."

Originally, Quakers gathered in any available space for periods of group silence. Followers waited for the Lord to exercise power over their lives and to provide answers about how to relieve world suffering. Anyone who felt that God had given them a message was encouraged to break the silence and speak. Today, Quakers are known worldwide for their humanitarian efforts and concern for quality education. Quakers continue to reject war and continue to stress the importance of peace.

The Moravians

The Moravians are another group that has contributed to the rich tapestry of the Pennsylvania German culture. The roots of the Moravian faith, under the leadership of John Hus, date to before the Protestant Reformation. This faith is regarded as the most ancient of Protestant religions still in existence. Members of the Moravian faith, originally called The United Brethren Church, were active in foreign missions long before other Protestant church groups.

Tenets of the religion include infant baptism, opposition to oaths, and the right not to bear arms. The Moravians suffered great persecution and were nearly annihilated before Nicholas Lewis, the Count Zinzendorf in Saxony, invited survivors to his estate for reorganization. He was a zealous Christian, impressed by Pietism and moved deeply by the Moravian's emphasis on Christ's sacrificial death as a blood atonement.

Once at the estate, Moravians built the village of Herrnhut, which housed 300 members. As time passed, the Count could not guarantee religious freedom in Saxony. He looked to America for religious freedom. Bethlehem, Pennsylvania was established as a Moravian community in 1741. For a span of 100 years, anyone could visit, but only Moravians could stay. The Moravians went on to develop Nazareth and Lititz as other towns in which members could practice their faith.

Moravians work for the benefit of each member of the faith. They were the first to initiate extensive missionary work with the Native Americans of Pennsylvania.

Chapter 2

The Pennsylvania German Dialect

The Pennsylvania Germans developed a dialect of their very own, commonly known as "Pennsylvania Dutch." This dialect originated within the languages spoken by Germanic groups located between Switzerland and Coblentz (the area now referred to as southern Germany). Through the course of its development, Pennsylvania Dutch has assimilated words with origins in English, French, Scotch, and Irish. For example, the Pennsylvania Germans are famous for shoo-fly pie. This molasses-based pie has a covering of crumbs that resembles the florets of the cauliflower. The word *shoo-fly* is derived from the French word *choufleur*, or "cauliflower."

Form was of no concern to the Pennsylvania Germans. They developed their language for the purpose of expressing ideas and for the convenience of passing time. Today, the dialect still thrives among some groups of Pennsylvania Germans; for other groups, remnants of Pennsylvania Dutch words and expressions remain a part of their everyday language.

There are many who think of the Pennsylvania Dutch dialect as being antiquated and unusual, but such is the case for any language deeply rooted in history, tradition, and beliefs. It is not uncommon for any cultural group to retain words and expressions that are not particularly correct in formal language. These words and expressions become a rudimentary part of one's informal language, perhaps for a lifetime. Many Pennsylvania German offspring did not find out until they reached a college or university English class that "outen the lights" was not the usual way to say "turn off the lights."

It was Martin Luther who refined and promoted "High German," which gave rise to the German language as we have come to know it today. But it was the early Pennsylvania Germans who nurtured the intrinsic heritage of a dialect that lives today in the hearts of those who reside in, or visit, the heartlands of the Pennsylvania German culture. The Pennsylvania Dutch dialect directly clarifies the premise that language is a birthright.

"Unknown Gentleman," watercolor on paper. Jacob Maentel (1763-1863?) c.1820 (10-5/8"x8-1/4"). (From the Permanent Collection of Franklin and Marshall College, Lancaster, Pennsylvania, The Leonard and Mildred Rothman Gallery)

Chapter 3

Family and Home Life

The Pennsylvania Germans cherished the family and took special pride in their homes. The family was a source of strength and great joy. Families considered children to be a blessing and desired large families. An average couple might have raised ten children. People loved and respected the older generations as well. Both parents and grandparents might live with a young couple or family. In some families, separate houses, or houses connected to each other, provided homes for the younger and older generations.

Family

Each family member assumed some of the responsibilities of maintaining the home. This was especially important to the survival of a self-sustaining household. The father was the central figure in the family. He made the important decisions concerning finances and education. Sons were apprenticed to their fathers and learned about farming, craftsmanship, and business. Girls were educated by their mothers to master the arts of the housewife. Making and mending clothes, housework, gardening, cooking, and cleaning flax were considered essential abilities if a girl was to be chosen as a wife and as a contributor to a self-supporting household. Spinning and quilting became important social outlets for these women.

Home

The Pennsylvania German home, the center of family life and work, was all-important. Before the Revolutionary War, Pennsylvania Germans were busy clearing the land. Their homes were simple, yet immaculate. Most were small homes built from the field stone readily available to the builder. Some were small log cabins, a sturdy dwelling familiar to early settlers from the Black Forest region and the Swiss Alps. The builder squared the logs with exact notchings so that they fit together at the corners. Families often built these small cabins into the hillside, near a spring, and they blended into the landscape as if they had "grown" there.

In time, families attached larger houses to the smaller stone houses or log cabins. The larger houses and the large barns did not appear until the land was cleared. This happened several generations after the first settlers arrived. The largest and most elaborate farmhouses were built during the late 1700s and in the

Benjamin F. and Lizzie H. Leaman. Wedding photograph of Benjamin F. Leaman (1879-1953) and Lizzie H. Denlinger (1880-1976). Of the Mennonite faith, they were married at Fertility, Lancaster County, Pennsylvania in 1901. (Courtesy of Carol E. Leaman)

1800s, a time of prosperity for the Pennsylvania Germans. The oldest brick house dates to about 1760, but by 1775, practically every building was built with stone.

Pennsylvania Germans were known for their comfortable and warm homes. They started using stoves for heating long before the rest of America adopted this form of heating. Their practice of building the chimney in the middle of the roof (instead of at the gable ends) and placing a five-plate stove, with the back plate missing, against a wall with a hole leading to the back of the fireplace allowed one stove to heat two rooms. These five-plate stoves were made in Pennsylvania as early as 1726 and were adapted from a stove that originated in central Europe. Eventually, a back plate, a door for wood, and a stove pipe were added. The stove was then moved to the middle of the room. Later, an oven was added to the stove—and the first cookstove was invented. However, some families continued to cook over an open hearth until the middle of the nineteenth century.

The kitchen, usually large with many windows to let in sunlight, became the gathering place for the family. Many of the household chores were performed on a large sawbuck table positioned near the fireplace. This fireplace was used for heating as well as cooking. The furniture was simple and utilitarian. Usually, there was a table and chairs, large Dutch cupboards for storing dishes, carved boxes that held salt and eating utensils, and perhaps a rocking chair in the corner. Often, a hanging cupboard off in the corner

contained the family Bible. Everything had its use and place; nothing was "for fancy." The floors were covered with braided rugs, and walls were decorated with calendars.

The bedchamber generally was dominated by a four-poster bed with a straw sack mattress resting on a rope-laced bed frame. Homemade feather-filled pillows, comforters made of homespun linen or wool, and colorful coverlets or quilts served as bed linens. Floors were mostly bare, but the rooms were always swept clean and kept uncluttered. Dower chests and Schranks (large wardrobes) as well as open dressers were used to store clothes and linens.

Pennsylvania German furniture consisted of two types: the rough, yet functional furniture of the early settlers, and the folkart decorated furniture of the nineteenth century. Many of the early pieces were crude and clumsy, reminiscent of medieval times. The early settlers were too busy clearing the land and building their farms to take time to build elaborate furniture. During the eighteenth century when Pennsylvania Germans had more time to think about furnishing their homes, several generations had gone by and much of the furniture styles popular in Europe had been forgotten. The most popular furniture during this period was to be found in Philadelphia. There, in 1725, cabinetmakers had begun to make Windsor chairs. Although the origin of the rocking chair is unknown, the earliest examples are from Pennsylvania.

It wasn't until the early nineteenth century that Pennsylvania Germans began painting their furniture. Painters of furniture, much like painters of hex signs (decorative designs on barns), traveled from farm to farm within a relatively small area. Thus, each area developed its own specific designs. Initially, only dower chests and bride boxes were decorated, but the custom soon spread, and dough trays, settees, chairs (especially rocking chairs), cupboards, and grandfather clocks were also painted. During this Victorian era, it was completely un-Victorian to paint furniture. Yet it was at just this time that adding a splash of color became important to the Pennsylvania Germans. They liked the color red and frequently used it in their homes. Houses were sometimes made from red brick, barns were painted red, and even roofs were painted red! By 1840, stencils had come into

Fractur (Birth Certificate). (Courtesy of Henry J. Kauffman, Professor Emeritus, Millersville University of Pennsylvania)

wide use, and it was no longer necessary to have an artist paint one's furniture. Popular stencil designs included the distelfink, fruit, flowers, and formal scroll designs. As the Pennsylvania Germans became more assimilated, they often adapted designs taken from other cultural groups.

Schrank. (Courtesy of Henry J. Kauffman, Professor Emeritus, Millersville University of Pennsylvania)

Barns

As the Pennsylvania Germans became more established in southeastern Pennsylvania as farmers, they began building their barns from stone. The barn was usually the biggest building on the farm. If possible, the barn was built into a hillside so that a farm wagon could enter directly onto the barn floor, which was located on the second floor. The animals were stabled on the first floor. A large, overhanging roof protected the animals from bad weather. The forbay always faced away from the wind. Pennsylvania Germans took good care of all their possessions, and this included the barns, which were swept clean regularly.

Several superstitious beliefs have been associated with Pennsylvania German barns. In some areas, geometric designs known as "hex signs" could be found on barns. In Europe during the middle sixteenth century, it was believed that these signs would keep away lightning and evil spirits. People have associated this belief with the hex signs painted on barns in Pennsylvania. However, in Pennsylvania these signs were used "just for fancy" (meaning "for decoration only"). Sometimes, a popular design such as a six-pointed star, a rosette, or a distelfink was painted directly onto the barn. Today, artists continue to develop new designs, always remaining true to folkart style. Many of these new hex designs have been copyrighted.

Another superstition associated with Pennsylvania German barns was the practice of using white trim on the doors of a red barn. These were called "the devil's doors," and folklore suggests that, to keep the devil from entering the barn, it was necessary to paint a white line around the barn door, much higher than the door itself. When the devil sees a door painted in such a fashion, he will leave and never come back. Windows with lines painted around them were called "witches' windows."

Cooking

The cooking and recipes of the Pennsylvania German housewives have become legendary. These resourceful people brought with them the best of cookery from their individual homelands and adapted them to the American experience. The Pennsylvania German housewife had to become resourceful and creative in many aspects of daily life, and this became especially evident in the recipes that she developed. The food skills of the Pennsylvania Germans were extensive, and remain extensive to this day. Anyone who has ever feasted upon sand tarts, pretzels, schnitz and knepp, shoo-fly pie, red beet eggs, apple butter, and chicken pot pie can verify this expertise.

The Pennsylvania Dutch cuisine was based upon a farming technique. The life of the Pennsylvania German required foods that could be stored during the winter months. Housewives had to gather foods from gardens and from fields and combine them with ingredients for preserving, drying, and storing. They learned to preserve, pickle, cure, spice, and can a variety of foods. A special favorite was "schnitz" (dried apples).

The main dish for most meals was soup, another custom transplanted from Europe. Housewives came forward with such favorable soups as potato soup, pretzel soup, calf's head soup, and chicken corn soup.

Pennsylvania Germans were their own butchers. Tasty, varied dishes using every available animal product were developed with great ingenuity. Meat pies, pot roast, pork and sauerkraut, and scrapple were favorites. Few vegetables and fruits were available in the winter. Therefore, the people mostly ate cabbage, dried corn, pickled eggs, egg custard, and cornmeal mush during these months. In the spring, a popular dish was (and still is) dandelion salad with hot bacon dressing.

Flour, a staple, was used for making dumplings, fritters, and pancakes. Dumplings were made from liver, potatoes, corn, and rice and added to many dishes. Buttermilk pancakes and fritters made with corn or apples were specialties served frequently.

The Pennsylvania Germans were responsible for developing earthenware pie plates called "Boi Schissel," which became the "dutch oven" technique popular today. The Boi Schissel helped to create the Pennsylvania German

fruit pies that have universal appeal. The Pennsylvania German housewife experimented with a variety of fruits when making pies. Some of the pies unique to Pennsylvania Germans were green tomato pie, apple pie, shoo-fly pie, cherry pie, pumpkin pie, and mincemeat pie.

Cakes, cookies, and bread continue to be extremely popular. Cake and cookie specialties were baked for every event and holiday. Coffee cakes and crumb cakes could always be found in the kitchen. Bread, especially pumpernickel, was always served with an added treat—jams, apple butter, and cheese spreads.

It is easy to understand why the legendary Pennsylvania German cooking can be found today beyond the borders of Pennsylvania. The history of these foods and their place in folklore adds to the rich heritage engendered by the Pennsylvania Germans.

Butter Mold. (Courtesy of Henry J. Kauffman, Professor Emeritus, Millersville University of Pennsylvania)

Chapter 4

Occupations

*T*hough farming was the most important occupation in the Pennsylvania German culture, it was not the only occupation. Many of the early settlers were craftsmen, such as weavers, hatters, brickmakers, potters, glass blowers, silversmiths, and iron masters. Pennsylvania Germans developed manufacturing centers and created items that were widely used by all settlers.

Farming

*F*arming was one of the major occupations of the Pennsylvania Germans. They developed self-sustaining farms and purchased almost nothing. They raised or manufactured on the farm everything that they needed. They grew food to provide for the family; but, being thrifty and industrious, the Pennsylvania German farmers sold or traded any surplus food. Bartering was an important activity among the farmers because money was not plentiful. For instance, farmers would barter produce for the products of craftsmen. Farm markets such as those found in Lancaster, Reading, and Philadelphia developed as a result of the money obtained from selling surplus food. Wagons went as far as fifty miles from home to sell produce and food items. The Pennsylvania German housewife was vital to the production and marketing of farm goods. She personally went to the marketplace, became known by the customers, and made sure that the foods being sold were pure and fresh. The family personally manufactured, transported, and sold their products.

*T*he Pennsylvania German farmer modeled many farming techniques after those used on The Palatine farms. In turn, many farmers in the new world modeled their techniques after those used by the Pennsylvania German farmers, who knew how to pick good land, conserve fertility, and increase productivity. The signs of good farming land were the presence of limestone rock and walnut trees! The use of manure and the rotation of crops were other innovations introduced by the Pennsylvania Germans.

*P*ennsylvania German farmers relied upon certain beliefs and superstitions contained in almanacs, which were handed down by word of mouth, to decide when to plant certain crops and when to harvest. Farmer's almanacs are still published in Lancaster, Pennsylvania and in Baltic, Ohio (in English, as well as the standard German). Many still turn to it for guidance. For example, a recent edition advised that spring onions should be planted on March 17th. The "why" seems to have had something to do with the moon and zodiac signs. The phases of the moon and the signs of the zodiac were important to life and to farming. Young children were taught the signs of the zodiac at their mother's knee, and wall hangings depicting the moon and the zodiac information were found in many homes. For whatever reasons, the Pennsylvania German farmers excelled in farming and raised plentiful crops for their families and for the community at large!

Woodworking

Woodworking was a necessary occupation for the Pennsylvania Germans. The men were skilled not only in building homes and barns, but in creating the furniture and articles needed in homes and barns. Home furnishings were mainly utilitarian. Woodworkers made large pieces of furniture such as cupboards (to store clothing and dishes), cradles, chairs, and blanket chests. Woodworkers also made kitchen items, which included butter and sugar molds, springerle molds, rolling pins, dough trays, candle boxes, and spice boxes. Most of the kitchen items were decorated with either carved or painted designs.

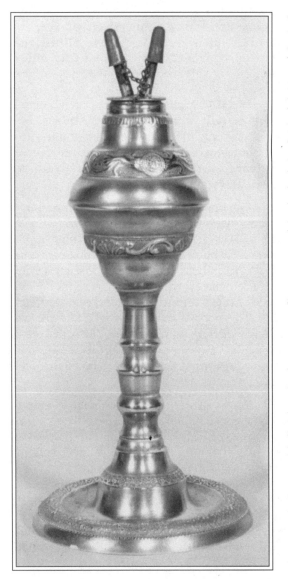

Pewter Oil Lamp. (Courtesy of Henry J. Kauffman, Professor Emeritus, Millersville University of Pennsylvania)

Weaving

Weaving was an occupation in the home as well as a profession outside the home. Cloth for everyday use generally was woven at home on a small handloom. Larger items were woven by professional weavers. Flax was woven into linen and added to wool to make a type of cloth known as "lindsey-woolsey." Cotton was also popular for weaving, by itself or after mixing in flax or wool. Pennsylvania Germans reserved wool for their "Sunday clothes." They reserved unpurified linen for the covers of the Conestoga wagons.

Indigo was the most commonly used dye. It was purchased from a peddler or country store and mixed with urine in dye pots. Other dyes included orange, from sassafras bark; a rich red, from pokeberries; and a red-brown, from walnut hulls. Thirty to forty bleachings were necessary to achieve a white color on homespun linen. Designs became popular—a double-woven woolen coverlet with a snowflake, or pine tree in traditional blue and white, was a favorite. As time passed, designs became more intricate and elaborate, incorporating trees, flowers, and birds.

Punched Tin Pie Safe (Pennsylvania). (Courtesy of Henry J. Kauffman, Professor Emeritus, Millersville University of Pennsylvania)

Manufacturing

Germantown became the first of several important manufacturing centers, followed by Lancaster, York, and Reading. Manufacturing developed in so many towns because of the difficulties of traveling long distances. It became necessary for each settlement to make its own cloth, iron, and glass—or else try to make do without such necessities. Most of these early factories were small; but once started, the manufacturers realized that their location in the heart of the English colonies was advantageous for trade. Thus, manufacturers began their efforts to find ways to get the products to Philadelphia, which became one of the great ports of the eighteenth century.

Iron

One of the very first industries in America was the manufacturing of iron. Pennsylvania was rich in iron ore—so rich, in fact, that it was not necessary to mine the ore. Pennsylvania Germans simply dug it from the ground! Many of the forges made stove plates for the stoves used to heat Pennsylvania German homes. Firebacks, pots, kettles, iron for blacksmiths, and the Franklin fireplace (known as the "Pennsylvania fireplace") were manufactured in Pennsylvania.

Many of these "iron plantations" were small communities in themselves. In addition to forge and charcoal centers, there was a mansion for the iron master, homes for the workers, a blacksmith shop, a barn, a store, and sometimes a grist mill and a saw mill. Farming, to provide food for the workers, was also present. Highly skilled labor was needed at the forge (or furnace), although the number of iron workers hired to keep the furnaces running was not large. To make sure a supply of charcoal was readily available for the furnaces, woodchoppers, colliers, and teamsters were also employed.

Tin Quilt Template. (Courtesy of The Schaeffer Collection from the Permanent Collection of Franklin and Marshall College, Lancaster, Pennsylvania, The Leonard and Mildred Rothma Gallery)

Chapter 5

The Conestoga Wagon

animals were capable of hauling eight tons and were one of the most notable breeds ever produced on this continent. Pennsylvania Germans permitted the breed to become extinct when the Conestoga wagon became obsolete.

A major contribution of the Pennsylvania Germans was the Conestoga wagon, the greatest of all American wagons. These wagons were first made in the Conestoga Valley, near Lancaster, Pennsylvania. Initially, Pennsylvania Germans used them to transport food from their farms to the towns. Later, the early pioneers used these wagons to carry their belongings.

*T*he Conestoga wagon was a sight to behold, and a marvel of Pennsylvania German construction. This great wagon, together with its huge horses, was often more than sixty feet in length when pulling a heavy load. Generally, the wagoner used a team of six horses (never less than four, nor more than eight) to pull the wagon along even the roughest of roads. Pennsylvania Germans bred special horses in the Conestoga Valley to pull these awesome wagons. The exact lineage of the breed is unknown. These horses stood 16 to 17-1/2 hands high and weighed close to 1,600 pounds. These powerful

*T*he wagons were boat-shaped, with slanted ends and a sag in the center of the wagon bed so that the load being carried would settle toward the center when the wagon shifted. The heavy rear wheels were 5-1/2 to 6 feet across. Eight to twelve hickory bows slanted upward and outward to form great arches that supported a homespun canvas top. The overhang of the canvas in front and back served to keep the rain from getting inside. The wagon frame was made of seasoned white oak. The axles were made from single hickory trees. The wagon body was painted blue; the wheels, running gears, and sideboards were painted vermilion (bright red); the ironworks were black; and the homespun canvas top was white. The harnesses on the horses were black, as were the bear skins covering the horses during winter. Every small detail of the wagon was enhanced with color.

*W*agon accessories included a wrought iron toolbox on the left side of the wagon, a red bucket hanging beneath the wagon, a black tar box, a blue feedbox, and a red wagon jack. For a final touch, each wagon was equipped with "team bells," warning other travelers on the road that a wagon was approaching. Tradition required that if a driver became stuck in mud and needed help, he had to give his bells to the man who helped him out of the mud. This is the origin of the sayings "Come home with your bells" and "I'll be there with bells on." These and many other colorful expressions still used today derived from the Conestoga wagon and their drivers.

An interesting feature on the Conestoga wagon was a "lazy board" made of white oak that could be pulled out on the left side of the wagon. The lazy board was strong enough to bear the wagoner's weight. Sitting on this board, the driver could operate the brake. Sometimes the wagoners walked beside the wagon or rode on the left rear horse so that he could reach all the other horses with his whip held in his right hand.

It was because of the Conestoga wagoners that Americans drive on the right side of the road. When a wagoner met a coach or another type of wagon, he pulled to the right to avoid sideswiping the other vehicle. Because the Conestoga wagon was so large, when a wagoner decided to drive on the right, everyone "decided" to drive on the right!

The Conestoga wagoners were a hearty breed of men. They are famous for the brief tall tales they would tell at stopover points along their journeys. These tales, filled with entertaining exaggerations, continue to amuse audiences today.

Conestoga Wagons. (Courtesy of Henry J. Kauffman, Professor Emeritus, Millersville University of Pennsylvania)

Chapter 6

The Pennsylvania Rifle

Another fine example of Pennsylvania German manufacturing was the Pennsylvania rifle. This rifle later became known (famously) as the Kentucky rifle because it was used on the frontier by such early pioneers as Daniel Boone.

Early German immigrants brought to Pennsylvania a rifle designed by Gaspard Kollner in Vienna around 1500. The true Pennsylvania rifle was a derivative of Kollner's design made by the gunsmiths in Lancaster, Pennsylvania. The gunsmiths greatly improved the rifle, giving it a longer barrel, greater accuracy, and a longer range. Weighing between seven and nine pounds, this 55-inch-long rifle made a very effective hunting weapon. Many decorated their Pennsylvania rifles with ornate designs. Some of these rifles, considered to be works of art, are collected or housed in museums. Mountings were made of intricately engraved brass. Some models even had inlays of silver.

Pennsylvania Rifles (gunsmith shop—Landis Valley Museum). (Courtesy of Henry J. Kauffman, Professor Emeritus, Millersville University of Pennsylvania)

Chapter 7

Folk Arts

The Pennsylvania Germans are well known for their folk arts—art made by the people, for the people. Some consider this folk art to be naïve and gaudy, but it originated because the Pennsylvania Germans wanted to add color to their everyday lives. Though many of the Pennsylvania Germans dressed plain, they still wanted the things they used to be colorful and pretty. They expected no financial gain from their folk art. It was "just for fancy."

Pennsylvania Germans painted familiar, everyday objects such as chairs, cupboards, chests of drawers, tin trays, and coffee pots. They made cookie cutters shaped like rabbits, chickens, hearts, houses, and stars. Geometric designs, birds, hearts, and flowers were popular motifs found on pottery, tinware, and needlework. The tulip was the most popular motif, followed by the heart. The most popular birds were the distelfink (which resembled a goldfinch), the peafowl, and a small parrot.

Many of the folk arts are still practiced today and can be found at craft fairs and in specialized craft businesses. Among the more popular folk arts are scherenschnitte, fractur, quilts, needlework, tinware, pottery, and basketry.

Scherenschnitte

Scherenschnitte is the folk art of scissor cutting. The Pennsylvania Germans brought this ancient tradition with them from Europe. Some of the cuttings were a form of home entertainment, and children took part in the art. Pennsylvania Germans used cuttings to illustrate love letters, New Year's greetings, and birth certificates, and to commemorate other important occasions. They also used cuttings to decorate the home. They made shelf linings from newspapers, and mantel decorations from thin, white paper, which was placed on a dark blue paper background. Paper doilies could be found throughout the house—favorite designs included hearts, birds, flowers, and scalloped edgings. This folk art is still practiced today by many artisans. All one needs is a pair of scissors, a piece of paper, and imagination.

Squirrel Cage. (Courtesy of Henry J. Kauffman, Professor Emeritus, Millersville University of Pennsylvania)

Fractur

Fractur is the decorative art of calligraphy. The term *fractur* is a Pennsylvania Dutch word meaning "illuminated writing." Fractur is recognized for its use of scrolled letters and for its unique illustrations—foliage, mermaids, sea horses, lions, quails, hummingbirds, angels, and human figures.

Derived mostly from religious works, the Pennsylvania German form of fractur presents a more "worldly" illumination of designs taken from daily life. Pennsylvania Germans used quill pens, homemade ink, and watercolors. Fractur was used primarily to decorate important certificates such as Geburtscheins (birth certificates), Taufscheins (baptismal certificates), Trauscheins (marriage certificates), Haus-segens (house blessings), and family records. There were also Vorschriften (student-lesson), which presented the upper- and lowercase letters for the owner to copy. The owner included his or her name and a religious verse. Usually, school teachers and preachers lettered and painted these certificates. Sometimes, teachers made a fractur as a reward for a very good student. The Pennsylvania Germans would combine scherenschnitte and fractur to commemorate a special event. The art of fractur is considered an important folk art, though there are not many artisans who still practice it.

Quilting

Quilting became an important social event for Pennsylvania German women, and continues to be a social occasion today for many groups. The women held "quilting bees," which provided a forum for working on quilts and exchanging news. Mothers taught young girls the skill of quilting early in their lives and would make quilts as part of their dowry.

Quilting became an art form among Pennsylvania German women. They created colorful designs using every available scrap of fabric, even using clothing or linens that were worn out in places. "Crazy quilts" were made using scraps of material from many varieties of cloth. Women would trade squares of material to get more variety. Popular quilt designs were the star, baskets of flowers or fruit, birds, and acorns. Many quilts were given interesting names, such as *Star of Bethlehem, Wedding Ring,* *Turkey Tracks, Tree of Paradise,* and *Seven Stars.*

Needlework

Throughout history, women of different cultures have created needlework "samplers." The Pennsylvania German women were no exception. Girls learned the art of cross-stitch at a young age. Samplers provided an opportunity for self-expression as well as a means of recording a special event—or simply another chance to practice the art.

Perhaps the finest of all needlework done by the Pennsylvania German women can be found in their "fancy" show towels. Homespun embroidered towels were hung over the everyday towels for use by visitors to the home. Cross-stitch was used to create tulips, hearts, stars, peacocks, and distelfinks. The maker usually stitched her initials, and sometimes the initials of her true love as well.

Tinware

Originally, tin was scarce because it had to be imported from England. Before long, however, the Pennsylvania German craftsmen began to make their own tin. Thin sheets of iron were dipped into molten tin because a tin coating would keep the iron from rusting. This tinware was more acceptable to the people because it was lighter in weight and easier to solder and maintain.

At first, the tin was painted freehand. In time, a stenciling technique became the popular way to decorate tin. Designs recalled from Europe were painted on coffee and tea sets, trays, cream pitchers, and trinket boxes.

Eventually, some Pennsylvania Germans began "punching" their tin rather than painting it. They used perforations to create designs that would allow for light and heat on cold, dark days. They also used punched tin for the doors of pie cupboards, so that air could flow over the baked goods; this kept the food from getting moldy.

Pottery

Much of the Pennsylvania German pottery was plain, decorated only with simple, graceful lines and colorful glaze—warm shades of brown, red, yellow, orange, and green. Flower pots, apple butter crocks, and milk cans were usually left plain, but greystone jugs and crocks were decorated with a tulip design using blue paint.

Usually, Pennsylvania Germans saved their finest decorations for the pie plates. They used two decorating techniques. Following an ancient tradition dating from the thirteenth century, *sgraffitto* designs were etched into the clay with a quill. This allowed for more intricate designs, such as tulips, distelfinks, and peacocks. *Slipware* designs were formed by trickling a lighter-colored clay through a tube and onto a darker pottery surface. This produced a crude design in which a few clay "lines" represented a simple flower or an animal. Sgraffitto and slipware techniques are still practiced by many artisans.

Two types of dishware became Pennsylvania folk art by adoption. These were Gaudyware and Spatterware. Gaudyware was produced in England. It was an alternative to good porcelain, which was too expensive for everyday use for most people. Because it was rarely found outside of Pennsylvania German locales, people assumed that the Pennsylvania Germans were the ones who had crafted Gaudyware—so it came to be known as "Gaudy Dutch." Lush, freehand designs, such as doves, grapes, and roses, were found on bowls, teapots, small plates, pitchers, cups, and saucers.

Spatterware was also imported from England. This became the dishware used for special occasions and was extremely popular with the Pennsylvania Germans. The focal point of the pattern was surrounded by spattered paint, which adorned the edges of the dish. The producers in England created pieces that contained favorite Pennsylvania German motifs, such as the peafowl and the tulip.

Basketry

Baskets had many uses and were made from straw or wood. Straw baskets were usually used indoors. They were made by securing continuous coils of straw with pliable oak thongs. A popular coil basket was the bread basket, in which bread dough was placed to rise. Hampers with removable tops, for holding such items as dried apples, grain, and "piece patches" for quilting, were also made using the coil method.

Splint baskets, heavier than straw baskets, were made from white oak. This type of basket took a long time to make. Straight-grained oak was thinly sliced on the schnitzelbank (a bench used to shave wood) using a draw shave; then the oak slices were soaked to make them flexible. Splint baskets had many uses, from holding eggs to measuring grain.

Chapter 8

Holidays

*F*or the Pennsylvania Germans, holidays represented a break in the daily activities. Many customs and traditions associated with special holidays were brought to America by the German-speaking people, while others developed as settlers became familiar with their surroundings. Holiday celebrations have endured to the present generation. Some Pennsylvania German customs and traditions have become a part of the holiday celebrations of other cultures, while others have remained unique to the Pennsylvania German culture. Several important holidays, and the customs and traditions associated with them, are discussed within this chapter.

New Year's Day

*I*t was (and still is) customary among Pennsylvania Germans to welcome the New Year with a feast of pork and sauerkraut to bring good luck during the coming year. One might ask, Why pork instead of turkey? The answer can be considered symbolic: "A pig roots forward and the turkey scratches backward!" (Yoder, *Discovering American Folklife*, p. 283). The Pennsylvania Germans have always taken great delight in making their own sauerkraut, which has probably become their trademark dish.

*N*ew Year's cakes, known as Springerle (see part III; page 102), were also a popular Pennsylvania German holiday custom. These large flat cookies (square or rectangular) had designs printed on them in relief using wooden molds or a rolling pin carved with designs that make cookie shapes on a single sheet of dough. Tradition says that the cookies go back to pagan times when, during a winter festival, people had to sacrifice animals to the gods. The poor, having no animals they could afford to slaughter, made token sacrifices with cookies that had animals on them. In time, other designs such as flowers, fruits, and human figures were used along with the animal images.

*A*nother New Year's Day custom for the Pennsylvania Germans, especially in rural areas, was "shooting in the New Year." Between midnight and sun up, a group of men would march to neighbors' houses and wish each household a "Happy New Year" by firing a volley of rifle shots. In addition to the rifle shots, one of the men would recite a wish (sometimes a rather long one) from memory. After these festivities, the head of the household would invite the guests to stay for refreshments. The custom of firing guns became so widespread that, in 1774, the Pennsylvania Assembly passed an act to suppress, on or

about New Year's Day, any disorderly practice of firing guns that disturbed the public peace.

On New Year's Day, many rural Pennsylvania German young people would dress in outlandish garb and ride into neighboring towns to "Whoop it up!" Known as "The Fantasticals," these young people would parade through the streets in carts, sleighs, or on foot. This custom later merged with the English custom of "mumming" (performing in elaborate costume and mask) and survives today in the form of the Mummers Parade, a New Year's Day celebration unique to Philadelphia.

Fasnacht Day (Shrove Tuesday)

The day before Ash Wednesday became known as Fasnacht Day among the Pennsylvania Germans. Fasnachts are a kind of doughnut, but without the usual hole in the middle. They are made from raised dough, deep fried and rolled in powdered sugar. Fasnacht Day was not a religious holiday, but rather one for festivals and dancing. Today, though, Pennsylvania Germans celebrate Fasnacht Day simply—by making and eating fasnachts.

On this day, it was customary to assign all household chores to the last person out of bed. This person, known as "die alt Fasnacht," was considered such a "disgrace" that children usually left their beds at the crack of dawn. A superstitious belief connected with this holiday required that the first three fasnachts be given to the chickens, to ensure that the chickens produce plenty of eggs. Pennsylvania Germans also believed that anyone who did not eat a fasnacht on Shrove Tuesday would suffer from boils.

Easter

Easter, a celebration of spring and rebirth, was primarily a religious feast to worship the risen Christ, and involved prayer services. This day, along with Christmas, was especially important to the Pennsylvania Germans.

Observance began on Maundy Thursday, when every good Pennsylvania German ate dandelion salad to ensure good health throughout the year. Maundy Thursday was followed by Good Friday (a sacred day of mourning), Easter Sunday, and Easter Monday. Easter Sunday was reserved for religious rites, while Easter Monday was a time for visiting family and friends, and no unnecessary work was to be done.

The Pennsylvania Germans brought the custom of the Easter Bunny and the Easter Egg to America. An old Teutonic legend claims that Ostara, Goddess of Spring and Fertility, transformed a bird into a rabbit around the time of the greening of Spring. In gratitude, the rabbit would forever lay eggs during the Spring Equinox, the feast of Ostara. Early Christian priests encountered this myth when introducing Christianity to the Germans. They incorporated it into the Easter observance, and the egg became a symbol for the regeneration of life in the spring.

Though today most Pennsylvania Germans are not acquainted with the Teutonic legend, most children (not just Pennsylvania Germans) grow up believing in the Easter Bunny, who hides brightly colored hard-boiled eggs on Easter morning. Customs involving the Easter Bunny vary from region to region. In some places children hunted for the eggs, while in other places they put hats under chairs and tables, as nests for eggs to be left in by the Easter Bunny.

An Easter game called "Picking for Keeps" was sometimes played with the colored eggs. Children would take turns holding up an egg by one end while another child hit that egg with the pointed end of a second egg that appeared to have a thicker shell. The winner was the child whose egg did not break. The famous "Egg Roll" that takes place on the White House lawn originated from this game.

Another popular custom associated with the Pennsylvania Germans is the custom of hanging decorated eggs' shells on small trees. A hole was made in both ends of the egg with a pin or needle. The egg was held to the mouth and the inside of the egg was gently blown out. The shells were then decorated with natural dyes. Egg trees became a source of great sentiment and memories, and people would save the eggs made by family members from generation to generation.

Ascension Day

Though primarily a religious day celebrating the ascension of the risen Christ into Heaven, for the Pennsylvania Germans, Ascension Thursday also had its share of superstitious beliefs. Pennsylvania Germans considered it bad luck to do work of any kind, especially sewing, on this day. For example, they believed that if someone swept the house on Ascension Thursday, ants would plague the household.

On this day, Pennsylvania Germans believed, certain plants were imbued with medicinal powers. People would collect these plants. They believed that tea brewed from the first 100 leaves gathered on Ascension Day would cure any ailment.

Harvest Home

Harvest Home is a Pennsylvania German festival usually held in late September on the Sunday nearest the feast of Saint Michael on September 29th. This festival was probably adapted from Autumn Ember Days, which was celebrated by German-speaking peoples in Europe. Religious in nature, Harvest Home was a time to thank God for his goodness at harvest time. Celebration usually consisted of a church service and sermon. Churches were decorated with the fruits, vegetables, and grains of harvest. It is still observed in many places.

The Pennsylvania German's Harvest Home was a rival to the Puritan's Thanksgiving. For a long time, the Pennsylvania Germans did not recognize Thanksgiving because they did not feel that it suited the climate and latitude of Pennsylvania—the celebration of Thanksgiving did not coincide with the harvest-time in Pennsylvania. However, by 1900, Thanksgiving had become a part of the Pennsylvania German calendar (the last Thursday in November) as they became more and more acculturated.

Christmas

Christmas was an important holiday for the Pennsylvania Germans, who celebrated in America with customs that originated in Europe. Many of these customs are still prevalent today.

The first recorded Christmas tree was decorated in Strasbourg, France in 1608. The custom spread rapidly among the Protestant sections of The Palatine and Alsace. Because many of the Pennsylvania Germans came from these areas, it seems likely that they were responsible for introducing this custom to Pennsylvania. With the exception of the Plain People, the decorated Christmas tree remains a universal custom within the Pennsylvania German culture. People decorated their trees with cookies shaped like animals, strings of popcorn, and candles. They built lavish miniature landscapes beneath the decorated trees: villages, fields with streams and animals, and (eventually) trains were popular. Such decorations and miniature landscapes are still popular today.

In the Moravian towns of Lititz, Emmaus, Nazareth, and Bethlehem, people build the "Putz" (a nativity scene) beneath the decorated tree in place of a miniature landscape. This custom also has become widespread. While the word *Putz* literally means "decoration," to Moravians it denotes the nativity scene. After attending church on Christmas Eve, Moravians go "putzing"—that is, visiting friends to see their nativity scenes.

The character Santa Claus, a blending of Saint Nicholas of the Netherlands and Kris Kringle of Germany, migrated from The Palatine. Saint Nicholas visited good children on his feast day, December 6th, and left candy and small gifts. Kris Kringle brought gifts to good boys and girls on Christmas Eve.

The character Belsnickel, whose disposition is diametrically opposite the benevolent personality of Santa Claus, comes from Holland and areas of Germany. Belsnickel would come to punish naughty children. Though he gave children candy and nuts, Belsnickel also carried with him a bag full of wooden switches, which he would use to "switch" children for their naughtiness! Belsnickel is no longer a part of Pennsylvania German Christmas customs because his appearance was so frightening to children that it offset the spirit of the Christmas season.

Some of the beliefs about Christmas have disappeared from the culture, but folk stories that feature them are still popular. Many Christmas stories feature beliefs about Christmas Eve, including: cattle and other animals can speak; well water turns to wine for three minutes; and the Christmas Rose bursts into bloom for one hour, between eleven and twelve o'clock.

Chapter 9

Brauche and Hexe

*T*he Pennsylvania Germans held to many beliefs and superstitions that originated in the European countries from which the people emigrated. These beliefs and superstitions were still strongly entrenched in the culture during the beginning and middle of the last century. Some were still in vogue during the first half of this century. Two popular beliefs are embodied in the Pennsylvania Dutch words *brauche* and *hexe*.

Brauche

*T*o *brauche* is "to heal." The use of prayers, blessings, and other conjurations to bring about healing is rooted in pre-Christian folk medicine and Christian folk beliefs. The "braucher" (healer) was a respected member of the community. He or she was called upon not only to cure illnesses and maladies, but also to help rid the community or a family of a problem that they felt was beyond their comprehension or ability to solve. The braucher sometimes employed herbs and other plants in the healing process. Even today, descendants of the Pennsylvania Germans occasionally resort to the use of certain ingredients, such as mud, herbs, or other plants to procure relief from sickness or an uncomfortable condition, such as fevers, headaches, and sore throats. For example, a mother might use a mixture of honey and lemon juice to cure a child's sore throat, or she might put mud on a bee sting to relieve the pain. Pennsylvania Germans also employed brauchers to destroy hexes.

Hexe

*T*he term *hexe* refers to an outside evil influence or spell. Pennsylvania Germans believed that there were people who willingly allied themselves with the devil so that they could work evil in this world, and that these people used evil books to cast evil spells. One of those books was *The Seventh Book of Moses*. It was thought to be a book of particular power and evil. It was said that anyone who read from this book could bring forth the devil. The reader would then fall under the influence of the devil, becoming a servant for working evil on others; however, the book was nonexistent and only a superstition. This belief has disappeared from the culture, but many folk stories that feature hexes and the devil are still popular.

Part II

Folklore

Chapter 10

Childhood Rhymes

Here There Sits a Mouse

Here there sits a mouse; [*touch child's forehead*]
It's building a house.
Here there sits a fly; [*touch child's nose*]
It's building a bridge.
Here there sits a flea; [*touch child's chin*]
And goes like this. [*gently drop fingers to the child's throat and tickle it*]

Doo hoct die maus;
Un baut n haus.
Doo hoct die mick;
Un baut n brick.
Doo hoct der floo;
Un macht soo, soo.

This One Is the Thumb

[*Take the child's hand and count on the child's fingers
as the rhyme is recited.*]

This one is the thumb;
This one shakes the tree on
which grows the plum;
This one picks them up;
This one carries them home;
And this little rascal eats
them all up!

Des iss der dauma
Der schiddelt die blauma,
Der leest sie uff,
Der drawgt sie heem
Un der glee schellem fresst
sie all deheem!

Giddap, Giddap

Giddap, giddap, little horsey. [*bounce child on your knee*]
Every hour a mile.
Every mile an inn.
Say there, hand me out a drink of
whiskey.
Should you then fall in a ditch,
I'll have to say:
Bang! There you lie. [*slide child down your leg and onto the floor*]

Reita, reita, geili,
Alla schtunn e meili.
Alla meili n wattshaus.
Geb mer moll n schmawler raus.
Reitschda ivver der grawva,
Fallscht du nei, so muss ich sawa:
Bumps! Datt leischta drin.

Treating a "Boo-Boo"

When a child experienced a minor injury, mother administered a little "brauching" by gently circling the wound with a finger and blowing on it while reciting the words below. The German words almost defy translation.

Heal, heal, chicken droppings,
By tomorrow morning all the pain will be gone.
Heeli, heeli, hinkel dreck,
Bis marya frie is alles weck.

Seven Ingredients

The baker says
He who wants good cakes needs
seven ingredients:
Butter and lard,
Eggs and salt,
Milk and flour,
And saffron colors the cakes yellow.

Backa, backa, kucha,
Der becker hot geruufa
Wer will scheena kucha havva,
Der muss havva sivva sacha:
Budder un schmals,
Oier un sals,
Millich un meel,
Un saffron macht die kucha keel.

A Seasonal Rhyme

Maiden if you wish to get married,
Marry in May,
When the cherries are ripe,
And then I'll bake you a pie.

Meedel, wann der heira witt,
Dann heier du im Moi.
Wann die kascha tseidich sin,
Noo back ich dier en boi.

A Nonsense Rhyme

One gets wet when it rains;
When it snows one gets white;
When there is sleet there is ice;
And with bacon one catches the mice.

Wann's reert, macht's nass;
Wann's schneet, macht's weiss,
Wann's kisselt, macht's eis;
Mit schpeck fangt mer die meis.

Little Barbara (Rag Rhyme)

Little Barbara, little chicken mouth,
Little hay fork.

Bevali, shneveli,
Hoi geveli.

I Will Show You (Rag Rhyme)

I will show you!
Tearing off the palings,
Tearing down pears,
And biting into them,
And then throwing them away.

Ich vil dir mol veisa!
Globort op reisa,
Biera runar reisa,
Aw-beisa, un vek shmeisa.

Little Mare (Rag Rhyme)

Little mare, little bear, little garden gate
Chop house, chicken house
An old woman goes out
Picks out the best chicken.

Marli, barli gawrda darli
Hok haus, hingle haus,
Gat 'n aldi fraw nous,
Pikt's besht hingle raus.

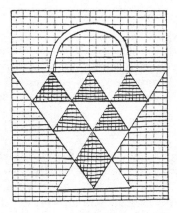

$\mathcal{A} \mathcal{B} C$

A, B, C,
The cat walks in the snow,
The snow goes away,
And the cat walks in the mud,
Jumps over the stumps,
With a bag full of rags,
Jumps over the barn
With a bag full of fire.

Aw, ba, za,
De kots lawft im shna,
De schna gat aveck,
De kots lawft in dreck,
Tshumpt ivar de shtumba,
Mit un sok ful lumba,
Tshumpt ivar de sheiar
Mit un sok ful feiar.

Counting Out Rhyme

One, two, three,
He, he, ha-ha, ho,
The miller lost his wife,
Seeks her with a little dog,
The little cat found her,
And the mouse sits on the house roof,
Bent entirely crooked with laughter.

Ans, zva, drei,
Hika, hoka, hei,
De milar hut sei fraw farlora,
Siecht se mit un huntli,
Sketsli hut sie g'funda,
Uns miceli hukt uf'm haus doch,
Un hut sich gons grum buklich g'locht.

Incantation to Call for Rain

[*Recite the words while knocking together stones held in both hands.*]

Rain, rain drops,
The boys we must paddle.

Raya, raya, drupa,
De boova mus m'r glupa.

A Riddle

A small iron horse,
A little linen tail,
The longer the little horse goes,
The shorter the little tail becomes.

[*Answer: Needle and thread*]

Eisich geili,
Leinich shwensly,
Ve linger's el geili gate,
Ve kartzer's es shwensly vart.

[*Answer: Nodel un nats*]

The Almanac Rhyme

The almanac that hung on the walls of Pennsylvania German kitchens was consulted daily. It provided many children with their first reading material—consisting not only of words, but also woodcuts portraying seasons of the year (this was the equivalent of a children's picture book). This rhyme alludes to the signs of the zodiac.

The weather butts; [*spring*]
The children are angry; [*spring*]
The lion roars; [*summer*]
The scales weigh; [*fall*]
The hunter shoots; [*fall*]
The watermelon pours; [*winter*]
The fish swims; [*winter*]
The goat leaps; [*winter*]
The scorpion crawls; [*fall*]
The maiden talks; [*summer*]
The crab scratches; [*summer*]
The steer moos. [*spring*]

Kallener

Der widder, der staised,
De kinner sin base,
Der labe, der brilled,
De woke, de gilt.
Der shitz, der sheeses,
Der wosser-monn geesed.
Der fish, der shwimmed,
Der shtine-buck shpringt.
Der scorpian shticht.
De yoongfraw shpricht.
Der greps, der shot.
Der us, der blot.

Sleep, My Little Darling, Sleep

This lullaby suggests a farm setting and is much beloved by Pennsylvania Germans. There are many variants to the lullaby, especially in the third line: the mother is always away from the home, but for a variety of reasons!

Sleep, my little darling, sleep,

Father is out watching the sheep.
Mother has gone to find the red cows
And won't be home much before morning.
Sleep, my little darling, sleep.

Schlofe, Bubbely, Schlofe

Schlofe, bubbely, schlofe,
Der dawdy heet de shofe.
Die mommy gate oon hold de rota key
Oon koomt net hame bis morriya free.
Schlofe, bubbely, schlofe.

(Sheet music for Schlofe appears on page 50.)

Schlofe, bubbley, scholofe, Der dawdi heet de schofe. Die

Mommy gate oon hold de rota key Oon koomt net hame bis

morriya free. Schlofe, bubbley, schlofe

Schnitzel bank

Iss des net en Schnitzelbank? Ya, des iss en Schnitzelbank.
Iss des net en Kaz und lang? Ya, des iss en Kaz und lang.

Kaz und lang, Schnitzelbank! Ei du scheeni ei du scheeni ei du scheeni Schnitzelbank!

Shaving Bench (A Nonsense Song)

Many verses can be added to this song—the more the merrier. This song holds a special place in the hearts of Pennsylvania Germans. Adults remember fondly the special people in their lives who led them in the singing of the "Schnitzelbank" (the "Shaving Bench" song.)

Refrain: Oh, you beautiful, oh, you beautiful,
              Oh, you beautiful shaving bench.

Verse: Is that not a shaving bench?
              Yes, that is a shaving bench.
              Is that not a short and long?
              Yes, that is a short and long,
              Short and long,
              A shaving bench.

[Refrain]

Verse: Is that not a little boy?
              Yes, that is a little boy.
              Is that not a little girl?
              Yes, that is a little girl.

[Refrain]

Schnitzelbank

Refrain: Ei, du scheeni, ei du scheeni, ei, du
Scheeni Schnitzelbank.

Verse: Iss des net en Schnitzelbank?
Ya, sell is en Schnitzelbank.
Iss des net en Kaz und lang?
Ya, sell is en Kaz und lang.
Kaz und lang
En Schnitzelbank.

[Refrain]

Verse: Iss des net en gleener Bu?
Ya, sell is en gleener Bu.
Iss des net en gleener Meedel?
Ya, sell is en gleener Meedel.
Gleener Meedel
Gleener Bu
Kaz und lang
En Schnitzelbank.

[Refrain]

From the Florence and John Burie Estate—origin unknown. (Courtesy of Audrey Burie Kirchner)

(Schnitzelbank continues on page 54.)

The Pennsylvania German. *Ed. J. William Frey, Pg. 7, June 2, 1949. (Courtesy of Millersville University Archives)*

Chapter 11

Plant Legends

St.John's Wort (Hypericum performatum)

St. John's Wort was called *Gottesblutt* in the Pennsylvania German dialect, meaning "Blood of God." This plant, brought from Europe, has leaves that appear to be spotted with blood; when crushed, the leaves produce a red juice.

According to legend, this plant grew beneath Jesus as he died on the cross, and drops of his blood fell upon its leaves. From that time on, the leaves of this plant have borne the blood of Christ. The name St. John's Wort arose from the belief that the plant would keep away evil spirits.

Rattlesnake Plantain (Epipactis pubescens)

The Rattlesnake Plantain is sometimes called *Verirrgaut*, meaning "Confusion Herb" in the Pennsylvania German dialect. It has dark leaves with white veins and grows in the woods. It is said that the plant looks very mysterious when come upon in the woods.

According to legend, when someone steps upon this plant, the person becomes wholly confused and does not know where he or she is. If this happens during the night, the person wanders aimlessly until morning, at which time the confusion lifts and the person's reason returns. If this happens during the day, something must shock the person back to reason. Some believed that a person could overcome the confusion by walking barefoot or by switching their shoes (right shoe on the left foot, left shoe on the right foot).

Lousewort (Pedicularis canadensis)

The Pennsylvania Germans have two names for this plant. Sometimes it is called *Widderkumm*, or "Come-Again Plant," and sometimes it is called *Lewesgraut*, or "Herb of Life."

According to legend, this plant's importance was discovered during the following course of events:

A long time ago, a beggar came to a farmhouse asking for food. A servant gave him a platter of food and a cup of coffee. When he went to the porch to sit down and eat, he encountered the master of the house sitting on a rocking chair. The master was an invalid. It seemed that even though this man's illness was gone, he could not regain his strength.

The two men began to talk. The beggar said, "You have been good to me. Because of this, I will bring you a plant that will give you back your strength."

When he had finished eating, the beggar went into the fields near the farmhouse and brought back the Lousewort. He told the master of the house that this was the "Come-Again Plant." He said, "If you use this plant by boiling the leaves and drinking the brew, you will regain your strength." The master of the house did as the beggar prescribed and his health and strength returned.

Swamp Pink (Sabatia angularis)

Swamp Pink was known to Pennsylvania Germans as *Dausengildegraut*, or "The Herb Worth a Thousand Guldens." As time passed, the "gilde" in *Dausengildegraut* became "gelde," changing the meaning to "The Herb Useful for a Thousand Ills."

According to legend, a colonel of a regiment once offered to make any soldier rich for life if that soldier could find an unfailing cure for the ills of the body. A brave young soldier searched the woods near the camp and brought back the Swamp Pink to the colonel. Because the colonel believed in the plant's healing powers, he granted the soldier one thousand guldens.

Devil's Bit (Chamaelirium luteumgray)

This plant is known as *Deiwelsabbisswazel*, or "The Root Bitten By the Devil," to Pennsylvania Germans. It was believed to have almost miraculous powers. The rootstock of this plant is short and thick. There is a legend as to how it came to be known as Devil's Bit.

According to legend, once, long ago, the devil became very agitated because people were not dying in great numbers. He wanted to know why, and soon discovered that people were using a certain root that had remarkable healing powers. The root had the power to remedy all the sicknesses that the devil had tried to inflict on people. To destroy the root, the devil tried to bite into it. But, because the root had been created by God, the devil was rendered powerless.

Pimpernell (Pimpinella saxifraga L.)

Pimpernell is an herb that the German-speaking settlers brought from Europe to Pennsylvania. For many years, Pimpernell was a popular garden plant used as a home remedy for fever, aches, and pains. It is called *Biewernell* in the Pennsylvania German dialect. Today this plant no longer exists.

According to legend, God allowed the curative powers of this plant to be revealed in a message from heaven to the people on earth. This message came during a time of great pestilence, when people were dying "like flies"; there was no known medicine or remedy. One day, a voice was heard coming from the sky: "Drink tea of pimpernell and you shall all get well."

Speedwell (*Veronica officinalis*)

The Pennsylvania Germans called the Speedwell plant *Ehr un Preis*, meaning "Honor and Praise." This plant was native to Europe, and the European culture from which the Pennsylvania Germans emigrated felt that it was important for men and women to honor and praise Speedwell.

The legend surrounding this plant tells of a shepherd who noticed that his sheep always ate the leaves of a certain plant as they began to graze. One day, he could contain himself no longer and ate some of the leaves. After doing this for several days, the shepherd felt stronger and healthier. He told others of his experience. Soon, the plant came to be known for its strengthening and curative powers, which deserved honor and praise.

This plant was found to have many applications. It was used as a tonic; a control for asthma, catarrhs, and coughs; a throat gargle; a way to promote menstruation; and a simple remedy for skin diseases.

Chapter 12

Tall Tales

The Bottomless Sinkhole

On the road between Catfish and Disston (now known as Oregon and Millport, respectively), there can be found one of many natural wonders of Lancaster County, Pennsylvania—a bottomless sinkhole. There are many stories and speculations that surround this hole, mostly dealing with the depth.

One day, quite a few years ago (no one seems to remember exactly when), there was a tramp walking along the road, admiring the pastures and wondering where he was going to find a place to rest that evening. As he passed the pasture that bordered the sinkhole, he noticed a cow grazing near the edge of the sinkhole. Soon, the cow wandered over to the hole and leaned down to drink. All of a sudden, the tramp heard a loud bellowing and looked up to see that the cow had slipped and fallen into the sinkhole.

The tramp could see that the cow was using all its strength to stay afloat, and he could see that the cow would not be able to get out of the sinkhole without help. So he started to run toward the distant farm buildings that were closest to the sinkhole, all the while calling for the farmer who owned the cow. After much searching, the tramp found farmer Miller working beneath a barn's forebay. Quickly, the tramp told him what had happened. The two men grabbed a long rope and rushed to help the cow.

When they got to the edge of the sinkhole, the cow was nowhere to be seen. Farmer Miller and the tramp could only  surmise what had happened to the cow—they thought that it had drowned and sunk to the bottom of the sinkhole. Farmer Miller became very upset because his cow was a valuable animal.

Several weeks went by. One day, farmer Miller was traveling toward Philadelphia to sell produce in the markets. Imagine his surprise when he spotted his cow! It had fallen through that sinkhole—all the way to Philadelphia! And, to his surprise, farmer Miller realized that his cow was not alone. It seemed that his cow had given birth to a calf somewhere along the way!

Everyone agrees that farmer Miller's cow somehow gave birth along the way, but many disagree on just where that cow fell out of the sinkhole. Some say New York. Still others insist that it was Philadelphia. Either way, farmer Miller got his cow back—and he got a brand new calf!

The Fish and the Fog

Old Herman had lived in Lancaster County, Pennsylvania, all his life. And, every day, just after daybreak, he would stroll down a path toward Little Conestoga Creek to say "Good Morning" to all the birds and fish.

On one morning in particular, as he strolled down toward the creek, the fog was so thick that he could not even see his hand when he held it out before him. Well, he almost turned around, thinking that perhaps he should not continue his usual walk to the river. But then he decided to go ahead—after all, he reasoned, he had walked this path every morning. He knew the path well. So, very slowly, he picked his way along, using his walking stick to feel for the edge of the path. He stumbled several times as he made his way toward Little Conestoga Creek. As he walked, he grumbled, "Dunderweather! This fog is so thick you could cut it with a knife!"

He wasn't far from the creek when, all of a sudden, peering through the fog, he noticed first a catfish—and then a perch and some suckers—swimming several feet (at the very least!) above the surface of the creek.

The reason the fish were swimming so high in the air, you see, was because of the fog—it was so-o-o thick that the fish swam from the water into the fog, not knowing the difference!

The Expert Farmer

Cyrus, a Pennsylvania German farmer, was a very good farmer. He was known far and wide for his wonderful crops, and many people sought him out for his advice on growing various plants.

One spring, Cyrus began to experiment with different kinds of fertilizers. He placed a broomstick in the ground at each spot where he scattered a sampling of each type of fertilizer.

Before long, he could not tell whether any one fertilizer was better than any other, nor could he remember which spot had which fertilizer. So you can imagine his surprise when, one day, he discovered that on two of the broomsticks that he had stuck in the ground, there were large ears of corn growing. On yet another broomstick grew a healthy potato vine. And two others had sprouted new brooms!

The Enormous Hog

Many years ago, Pennsylvania German farmers often bragged about the size of their hogs. One hog in particular is still remembered as being the champion of hogs! Old Harry was the farmer who raised this huge, fat, sloppy hog, and people would come from all parts of the county just to see this champion hog.

After many months, when it came time to butcher this champion hog, the only site that was large enough was the local dam. Men came out to watch the butchering, and soon found themselves volunteering to help. Why, it took at least ten men just to scrape the bristles from the hide of that hog!

Another group of men boiled the fat to make lard. When they had finished, they had a vat so large that when one man slipped and fell into the vat, he drowned!

When they finally finished with the butchering, this champion hog yielded more than fifty bushels of sausages, more than one hundred tins of pork pudding, and *two* stomachs! Inside those pig stomachs, the farmers discovered some additional surprises—a rake, a post-hole digger, and two milking cans!

Early to Rise

It is well known that Amish farmers arise early in the morning. It is said that they arise so early that they meet themselves going to bed.

A Wagoner's Well-Trained Horses

(The Conestoga wagoners were known for their very short stories that exaggerated aspects of their job and adventures.)

One evening, before entering a tavern, a Conestoga wagoner hitched his lead horses to a tree. He gave them a command to "Pull." When he returned to the tree the next morning, the horses were still pulling at the immovable tree because the wagoner had not given them the "Whoa" signal.

The Unusual Apple

Jacob, a Conestoga wagoner, stopped for a rest. He sat upon a log to eat an apple. Jacob pared the apple and stuck the knife into the log. What a surprise he had! The "log" was a huge, black snake. The snake suddenly slithered away—and Jacob was treated to a wild, free ride on its back.

A Wild March Wind

One March evening, when the weather was blustery, several Conestoga wagoners sat warming themselves near a blazing log in the fireplace of a wayside tavern. It wasn't long before they began bragging about their travels, each one trying to outdo the other's exploits.

One old wagoner sat and listened for a long while. Eventually, he was persuaded to tell about his travels. All eyes were upon him as he recounted driving his team of horses across the Allegheny Mountains between Carlisle and Pittsburgh.

He slowly stated, "This particular day was so fierce and windy, much like tonight, that I had to hire seven men just to hold my hat on my head!"

Chapter 13

Folktales

The Bear and the Fox

Percy, a farmer, and his wife, Lydia, sat in their farmhouse kitchen, very pleased with themselves. The special smell of sauerkraut filled the air around the farm! Weeks before, preparing the cabbages for fermentation, the couple had worked very hard. Today, three large tubs of their favorite food sat in the farmhouse cellar, ready to eat. They were planning a special sauerkraut dinner that evening for family and friends. But there was something that Percy and Lydia had not planned for: a fox and a bear had crept through the farmyard and entered the farmhouse cellar through an open window. The fox and the bear were feasting on the sauerkraut! The fox was a sly old fellow and he pretended to be the bear's friend, even though he did not like the bear.

When the fox had eaten his fill of the sauerkraut, he began to climb in and out of the cellar through the window. He was trying to get Percy's attention, who was still in the kitchen, so that the farmer would know what was happening in the cellar.

The bear asked the fox, "Why this jumping in and out the window?"

"I am watching to see if the farmer is awake," replied the fox.

The bear ate and ate. He became fuller and fuller and bigger and bigger. His stomach actually touched the cellar floor!

Then, all of a sudden, the farmer opened the cellar door! The sly fox took one more taste of the sauerkraut and escaped through the window. But the bear, whose paws were full of sauerkraut, had eaten so much that he became stuck in the window when he tried to escape. There he was with his head outside the cellar and his bottom inside the cellar. Percy took his paddle, spanked that bear, pulled him back into the cellar, and booted him through the door.

The bear and the fox were never seen again. But Percy and Lydia knew they were around because every time the couple went into the woods, they could smell sauerkraut!

Solly, the Blind Man and the Giant

Long, long ago, a lamb said to a blind man named Solly, "You are of no use. What can you do in the world?" Solly answered, "Come into the world with me and I will show you what I can do."

As their journey began, Solly offered to carry the lamb on his back. The lamb agreed and the two traveled until they came to a strange country. As they walked along a path through the woods, they found a donkey tied to a tree. Solly had decided that they should take everything they found along their journey. He put the lamb on the donkey's back and then climbed on the donkey's back behind the lamb. Solly and the lamb rode away.

As the journey continued, they found a plowshare, which Solly put on the donkey's back. When they had gone farther, the lamb saw a heavy rope and said to Solly, "I see a heavy rope on the road." The blind man replied, "Good! We will take it along."

By this time, it was growing dark and they had ridden into dense forest. Suddenly, in the distance, the lamb saw a great palace. Solly dismounted and put the lamb on the ground beside him. They walked to the door and Solly knocked. When no one answered, Solly tried the door. Finding it unlocked, Solly gathered all of their things and they entered, closing the door behind them and locking it.

Later that night, the King of the palace returned on his horse. When he tried the door, he found that it was locked. He knocked and said in a loud voice, "Who is in there?"

A voice from inside shouted, "Who is out there?"

The King answered back, "I am a giant."

From within, a louder voice replied, "The grandfather of a giant is in here."

At this, the King demanded to hear the voice of the giant's grandfather. Solly heated a bar of iron in the fire and struck the donkey with it. The poor donkey gave a loud, horrible bray.

Then the King said, "Surely, from the sound of your voice, you must be the grandfather of a giant, but to truly convince me, pull out one of your teeth and throw it out to me."

At this request, the blind man threw out the plowshare. The King roared, "To be very sure, I want you to throw me a strand of your hair." So, Solly threw out the rope.

Finally, the King declared, "By the sound of your voice and the size of your tooth and your hair, you are surely the grandfather of a giant. Stay where you are. The palace is yours for as long as you live." Then he quickly rode away on his horse.

Thus, the lamb and Solly acquired a beautiful palace and great wealth. And the lamb realized how truly cunning and wise his friend Solly was.

The Princess Who Would Not Laugh

Once upon a time, there was a king who had a daughter who would not laugh. Everything he tried was unsuccessful, and so the king proclaimed that he would give his daughter in marriage to any man who could make her laugh.

One young man went to a wise old woman and asked her what he could do to make the princess laugh. She gave him a ball of string and said, "Go to the house of the church caretaker and get him out of bed early in the morning while he is still in his night clothes. Give him the string and, when he is holding it, say: 'Hold and hold on.' He will have to follow you. Then go to the princess."

The young man did as he was told. He awakened the caretaker from his sleep, gave him the string, and said, "Hold and hold on." When the young man turned to go, the caretaker realized that he had to go with him. The caretaker yelled loudly and his daughters came running in their nightgowns to free him. But the young man said, "Hold and hold on," and they, too, had to follow him.

When the group went by the pastor's house, the pastor tried to free the caretaker and his daughters. But, again, the young man said, "Hold and hold on," and the pastor had to follow him.

The princess was looking out of one of the palace windows when the young man and his group arrived. She began to laugh so hard that she could hardly stop. The king kept his promise— the young man married the princess—and they lived happily ever after!

The Witch and the Broom

In a small village, there was a family and a woman who lived nearby. The woman visited the family frequently. They came to believe that she was bewitching one of the members of their family.

One day, the youngest son went to play with a new friend. He was surprised to see a broom lying across the doorstep. He said to his friend, "Why do you have a broom at your door?" The friend replied, "It is to keep witches away. Did you not know that a witch cannot step over a broom?"

The boy could hardly wait to tell his family the news. When he told them about the effect that a broom could have on a witch, the family devised a plan.

Finally, a few days later, the woman paid a visit. The youngest son ran to the cellar and hammered a nail in the ceiling directly under the chair in which the woman was to sit. He hung a broom on the nail. The family invited the woman to stay for a visit and she sat in the chair offered by the family. After visiting a short time, she tried to get out of the chair, but found that she could not. She talked a little bit longer and, once again, tried to get out of the chair.

The family smiled with success when the woman said, "If you remove the broom from beneath the chair, I will never bother any of you again." The boy ran to the cellar and removed the broom from the nail. At that, the woman returned to her home and never visited the family again.

The Three Horsemen

A long time ago, a family lived along a public road near Lancaster, Pennsylvania. While the mother and grandmother were tending the garden, two young children were sitting in the road making mudpies.

All of a sudden, the women heard a thundering noise and the screams of her children. When the mother and grandmother turned to look down the road, they saw to their horror that three wild horsemen were riding toward the children with lightning speed. The children became so frightened that they could not move.

"Oh, God! Help my children!" screamed the terrified mother. The three horsemen suddenly disappeared and all that remained in the road were three elderberry canes. You see, the three horsemen were witches—but the mother's cry for help had turned them into canes!

The Braucher

There was once a farmer whose cattle were noisy and restless at night in his barn. He went to see a person who could brauche.

The braucher promised the farmer that he would, that very same night, stop the evil one who was tormenting the cattle. But first he made the farmer promise to stay inside his house, no matter how much noise he heard coming from the barn.

That night, the cattle grew noisier than ever before. Finally, the farmer could not stand it any longer. Against the wishes of his wife, he left the house and went to the barn. To his surprise, the braucher was lying on the ground inside the barn.

"What are you doing here?" demanded the farmer.

"I am waiting for the witch," the braucher said.

At once, the farmer knew what was happening! "It was you all along!" he screamed. "You have been beating my cattle to make them noisy and restless. You have been coming night after night to my farm so that I would believe a witch was after my cattle, so that I would pay you money to stop the witch. Get away from here as fast as you can, and stay away!" With this, the braucher jumped up, ran away, and was never seen again!

In Days Gone By

There was once a rich, greedy miller. One day, two men who wanted to steal money from him came to visit. The men had found a copy of *The Seventh Book of Moses*. Many believed that one could call forth the devil by reading from this book.

When they reached the mill, one of the men quietly hid inside in a dark corner while the other entered the mill and approached the old miller, who was standing by his cider press. He said, "Old man, I have a book that can call forth the devil, who will make you rich. Shall I do so?"

"Go ahead," said the old miller cautiously.

"First you must lock the door," replied the man.

The miller locked the door. Slowly, the man opened the book. He began reading and then paused to say, "We are now at a difficult part."

He began reading again and then stated, "This is a very difficult part." Reading on, he paused to say, "I have now come to the most difficult part of all. The devil is about to appear before you. When he does, you must deal with him yourself."

As the man continued to read, he gave a signal to his partner. Suddenly, his partner ran out from the corner, pretending to blow a flame from his mouth. The old miller's eyes filled with great fear and, as his screams penetrated the old mill, he jumped right through a window frame, which stayed attached to him until he reached his home. He locked himself safely inside.

Standing together, the two men looked at each other. They shook their heads resignedly. Finally, one of them broke the silence and complained, "If only that old devil of a man hadn't run away from us—we could have gotten some money from him!"

Mother Rabbit and the Bear

Once upon a time, there was a white mother rabbit with four little baby bunnies, whom she loved very much. To keep them safe while she was away from the nest, Mother Rabbit warned the bunnies never to let anyone in who did not have white paws. She taught them to listen for these words when she returned to the nest with food:

> "My little paw is full of leaves,
> And my little nipples are full of milk."

The mother taught her baby bunnies to answer with these words:

> "Show us your paw."

Mother Rabbit would show her white paw and the young rabbits would let her back into the nest.

One summer day, a big brown bear, who had been watching and listening to the rabbit family, crept up to the nest while Mother Rabbit was away. He said, "My little paw is full of leaves, and my little nipples are full of milk."

The little bunnies answered, "Show us your paw."

When the bunnies saw the brown paw, they would not let the bear into the nest. They had listened well to their mother!

The big brown bear was not happy. Sitting under a tree, the bear thought and thought and thought. After a while, a plan came to mind. Hurrying to a flour mill, the big brown bear whitened a paw with flour and went back to the nest. He said, "My little paw is full of leaves, and my little nipples are full of milk."

The little bunnies answered, "Show us your paw."

The big brown bear showed the bunnies the whitened paw and they let that nasty bear into the nest. Once inside, the big brown bear swallowed the little bunnies.

When Mother Rabbit came home, she said, "My little paw is full of leaves, and my little nipples are full of milk."

The big brown bear growled, "Come in and I will swallow you, too."

Mother Rabbit became so frightened and upset that she ran away as fast as she could. When she thought she was safe, she slowed down and started to walk along a wooded path that led back to her nest. A dog came along. Mother Rabbit told the dog that a big brown bear had swallowed her babies.

After walking awhile with the dog, they met a cat. Mother Rabbit told the cat that the big brown bear had swallowed her babies. The cat joined Mother Rabbit and the dog in their walk along the path.

The three came upon a swarm of wasps. When Mother Rabbit told the swarm that the big brown bear had swallowed her babies, the wasps joined the group. They walked all the way back to Mother Rabbit's nest. Along the way back, many other animals who had heard the news joined the Mother Rabbit and the others, following behind them.

Once there, the wasps flew into the nest and began to sting the big brown bear. The bear fled the nest, but the wasps continued to sting him until he could not move. The other animals who had come with Mother Rabbit pounced upon him and kept the bear down on the ground.

Mother Rabbit cut open the bear's belly and found her four little baby bunnies, still alive! She thanked her animal friends and, after they had returned to their homes, Mother Rabbit and her babies went back to their nest. The rabbit family lived happily ever after.

As for the big brown bear, he ran away as soon as he could move, and was never seen again.

The Endless Story

Once a man named Hans was sentenced to death and he began to plead desperately for his life. His executioners talked among themselves and then presented Hans with a challenge. They said, "We will spare your life if you can tell us a story that has no end."

Hans agreed to accept the challenge, and this was the story he told:

> "A large room was filled with wheat. The only opening in the room was a small hole through which only a weevil could crawl. By and by, a lone weevil entered the room and carried away a grain of wheat. Soon, a second weevil came and carried away another grain of wheat. Soon, a third weevil came along and carried away—"

"Wait," cried the executioners, "There is no end to this story."
"Then set me free. Give me my life!" cried Hans.
The executioners kept their promise and set him free.

A "Distelfink" Story

(This is one of many stories that features the distelfink, a symbol for happiness, used as a design for many folk crafts. No one is really sure of the bird's origin.)

For a long time, Pennsylvania farmers had been troubled by a ruinous weed—the thistle weed. Little gold finches ate the seeds from the thistle weed and used the fuzz that lined the seed pods to build their nests.

Soon, the thistle weeds were no longer a menace, so the farmers came to think of the gold finches as good luck charms for their crops. They called them "thistle finches," which in the Pennsylvania German dialect becomes "distelfink."

The Curious Servant

Witches would often gather in fields and find spots that they called "Witch Rings." These were circular areas in the fields where nothing would grow.

Once, there was a man named Jake, who was a servant in a witch's house. As Jake watched one night, he saw the witch grease her feet with lard and stand before the fireplace. Jake heard her say, "Up the chimney I go and touch everything." Suddenly, she was drawn up the chimney!

When he thought that the witch was gone, Jake greased his feet with lard and stood before the fireplace. He said, "Up the chimney I go and touch everything." Jake, too, was drawn up the chimney, bumping from side to side all the way up!

He was whisked through the air and set down in a field where many witches were gathered. Jake shared a delicious meal with them.

At four o'clock in the morning, the cocks began to crow. Everything disappeared, and Jake was left alone with only a few old bones for company. Jake did not know where he was. He began walking.

As dawn approached, Jake realized where he was—and he realized that he was at least a day's journey from his home! When Jake returned to the witch's house late that night, he was scolded soundly. He promised then and there never to practice witchcraft again.

The Devil Cannot Do the Impossible

Three carpenters were tearing down an old log cabin. One of them found *The Seventh Book of Moses* hidden between some logs.

Later, while eating lunch, one of the carpenters wanted to read from the book. His fellow carpenters pleaded with him not to open the book. They said, "This is an evil book. Let us destroy it immediately."

"Why so?" asked the carpenter holding the book.

The older of the other two carpenters spoke. "I have heard that, as one reads deeply into *The Seventh Book of Moses*, the devil will appear and grant any wish to the reader. Then the devil asks the reader to sign a paper, after which the reader becomes a witch who has certain powers until death. Upon death, the devil takes back the powers."

But curiosity overcame the carpenter who held the book, and he began to read. As he read deeper into the evil book, the devil suddenly appeared before him and demanded, "What do you want me to do for you?" The carpenter froze with fear.

One of the other carpenters quickly grabbed an old bottle that had a broken bottom and said, "Fill this bottle with water as quickly as possible."

The third carpenter ran to find a braucher as the devil went to a nearby water pump and tried, unsuccessfully, to fill the bottle. The braucher arrived quickly and released the foolish carpenter from the devil's power by reading from his book of prayers. When the braucher destroyed the devil's book, the devil disappeared, and was never again seen in that area.

The Peg

A woman was walking down the lane of her neighborhood, carrying a basket of shiny red apples. She stopped to talk to a neighbor and her young child. The woman reached into her basket and handed the child an apple before continuing her walk.

Shortly after eating the apple, the child became very ill and began vomiting tacks and nails. The frantic mother screamed for her husband, who was working in the fields. When he found out what had happened, he quickly went to a braucher for help. The farmer told the braucher that he suspected that the woman was a witch.

"You are correct," said the braucher. "But I will end her spell on your child. Take this wooden peg. When you get home, bore a hole in a tree near the house, place the peg in the hole, and hit the peg several times with a hammer. This will cause the woman to experience much pain, and she will come to you and promise to stop bewitching your child in return for relief. "But," the braucher cautioned, "if you hammer the peg all the way into the tree, the woman will die."

The farmer returned home and followed the braucher's orders. But, as he was about to tap the peg into the hole, anger consumed him. He struck a mighty blow to the peg and drove it all the way into the hole. Realizing what he had done, he ran to the woman's house. He found the witch just as she drew her last breath.

The Dishonest Milkman

Every day, after Henner had milked his cows, he saved the milk his family needed and took the rest to a nearby town to sell or to use as barter. Henner always passed a creek and stopped there to pour water into the milk—so that he would have more "milk" to sell.

On one particular day, Henner took his milk to a woman who had always bought her milk from him. Lydia looked into one of Henner's pails and exclaimed, "Henner, there is a little fish swimming in the milk!"

Henner thought for a moment and shook his head up and down. With a sly smile, he said to Lydia, "Yes. The cows drank water at the creek this morning!"

The Eternal Hunter

One dark, cold winter night, a small group of men were clustered around the local store, discussing the weather. Suddenly, Jake suggested that it was a good time to hunt raccoons up on South Mountain. Now this particular night was very cold, and as the group looked up, they couldn't even see one star in the sky. Even the moon was hidden behind the clouds.

Clyde, the storekeeper, said, "Better stay at home. This night is not fit for man nor for beast. Tonight is a night for the Hunter, and woe to any man who crosses his path!"

Henry said, "Remember the legend. On a cold, still winter night such as tonight, the Eternal Hunter hunts with his pack of dogs. Anyone meeting the Hunter will be torn to bits by his dogs, or spirited away into the night. No one who has encountered the Hunter has ever been seen again."

Friends and families all talked at once, trying to convince the men not to go out. All but three men agreed not to hunt that night. But Johnny, Jake, and Ezra laughed at the people's fear of this mythical "hunter."

"We'll be back early," the three men promised as they mounted their horses, called for their dogs, and rode off into the dark night, heading toward South Mountain.

During the course of several hours of hunting that night, the men had little luck in locating any raccoons. The three men climbed a high ridge to listen for the sound of their dogs barking. Just as they were about to call for their dogs to return so they could start the journey home, they thought they heard something. Johnny, Jake, and Ezra were very still, listening. Then they heard it again—someone else was calling for dogs. To their dismay, they realized it was the Eternal Hunter calling for his dogs.

Holding their breath, they listened intently, trying to determine where the Eternal Hunter was. After several minutes, they decided the calls were coming from across the deep valley. They would have to cross this deep valley to get home.

Now all three men were quite scared, and each one jumped at the slightest sound! The men talked quietly, trying to decide whether it would be safer to hide until morning and hope the Hunter did not find them, or take a longer road that went around the valley to reach home. Suddenly, one of the men remembered their promise to their families. The men knew they had to try to reach home quickly or their families would come looking for them and very likely walk right into the path of the Eternal Hunter. So, taking a deep breath, they quietly called for their dogs.

The dogs came running, scared and skittish, as soon as they heard their masters call. As the men rode down the long road home, their dogs stayed close, trailing behind the group. They did not run ahead, as dogs usually do on a hunt.

Ezra said, "What do you think is wrong with the dogs? They are acting very strange for hunting dogs."

The three men had traveled for almost an hour along the road, when they saw a strange, black animal bearing its white teeth, blocking the road ahead of them. And then they knew—the Eternal Hunter was nearby!

Ezra, Johnny, and Jake halted the horses, shivering. They knew they had to act quickly if they were to escape the wrath of the Eternal Hunter. So they huddled close together, trying to decide what to do.

Suddenly, Jake noticed that the strange black animal seemed to be paralyzed by the light from their lanterns.

"Look!" said Jake, "It doesn't move at all. As long as we keep the lanterns in the direction of the animal, the beast won't attack. All we have to do is keep the light in its face." Then Johnny realized that there was another problem—he said, "But we only brought enough oil to last for a few hours. I didn't think that we would be out here this long. We have already burned most of our oil."

Quickly, the three men checked their supply and decided that they needed to move—and move now—if they were to make their way around the strange black creature before their lamps went out.

Huddled close together, keeping their dogs very near to them, the three men swiftly rode around that strange animal. Keeping their lanterns directly in front of the strange animal proved difficult, but they got past the creature at last and continued toward home. The animal remained frozen in its tracks until the last speck of light disappeared.

When Johnny, Jake, and Ezra finally reached home, it was almost daybreak. Their families were just beginning to form a search party to look for them. Everyone started talking at once. The three men took turns shouting about how they had just outsmarted the Eternal Hunter.

The Ghost That Would Not Be Mocked

One night, Sarah, Rebecca, and Rachel were returning home from the village store. The shortest way home was to pass the cemetery of Ebenezer church. Because it was getting late, they decided to take this shorter route.

When the girls came close to the cemetery, all three saw a light at exactly the same time.

Rachel announced loudly, "That is a ghost!"

"Be quiet," whispered Sarah and Rebecca, "at least until we have passed through the cemetery!"

But Rachel kept on talking, saying, "Ghost, come out and carry my dress through the mud!"

Quick as a flash, the light came toward the girls and began to follow them. The girls started to walk faster, and faster, and faster, but still the light came toward them. The faster they walked, the faster the light came toward them.

They crossed a meadow near their house, and still the light followed them.

At last they reached Sarah's home. They stopped on the porch to watch the light. It hesitated and then disappeared. They discovered, to their amazement, that Rachel's dress had been torn—so bad, in fact, that she could never wear it again.

The Ghost of the Cornerstone

Several years ago, Jake and Rachel had purchased a farm, unaware that years earlier the previous owner had removed the cornerstone of his farm and had placed it on land that belonged to his neighbor.

Not long after Jake and Rachel moved onto the farm, they became aware that there was a spirit that moved about at night along one of the boundary lines of their farm. Knowing that he had to do something about this ghost, Jake went into the village to seek the advice of someone who was known to have dealt with spirits.

The villager instructed Jake: "Go out at night and stand three paces away from the stake that marks the east back corner of your farm. Be sure to carry a silk handkerchief in your right hand."

When he reached home, Jake told Rachel what he had been told to do. She agreed that something had to be done about the ghost.

That night, Jake did exactly as he was told. Shortly after he had positioned himself three paces away from the east back corner of his farm, the spirit arrived.

As the spirit approached the stake, it moaned, "Where shall I put it?!"

Jake answered, "Dunderweather! Put it at the very spot where you got it."

The spirit sighed deeply and said, "For many years I have waited to hear those words. When I was alive, I quarreled with my neighbor about a boundary line. Then I pulled out one of the corner stones. All these years I have been wandering about seeking rest. Now I shall find it."

The spirit took the stake in its left hand, and held out its right hand as if to shake Jake's hand in thanks for what he had spoken. Jake held out his right hand while holding the silk handkerchief. When the spirit touched the handkerchief instead of Jake's hand, the handkerchief immediately turned to ashes. With that, the spirit disappeared.

The next morning, Jake and Rachel noticed that the stake had been moved to a different spot. They claimed this new spot as the original corner of their farm. The spirit was never seen again.

The Pot of Gold

Once upon a time, there was a very old man named Ezra. He and his wife, Sarah, lived on a farm far out in the country. They had lived on this farm for many years, ever since the previous owner had died. This previous owner was known to have gone thieving at night. He would take a little something from one place, or a handful of something from another place, but no one was ever able to find any of the items he had taken.

One day, old Willie, a tramp, wandered up to Ezra's farmhouse. "Please, can you spare some food?" asked old Willie.

Ezra told Sarah to give the stranger some food. After he had eaten, Willie asked, "May I sleep on your porch tonight?"

"Yah, but just for tonight," Ezra agreed. "It looks like rain."

Shortly after dark, Ezra and Sarah went to bed. The house became very quiet.

Around midnight, a sound awakened Willie the tramp. He listened carefully and heard a man's voice say over and over, "Where shall I put it? Where shall I put it?"

At first, Willie ignored the voice, trying to sleep, but the voice would not stop calling, "Where shall I put it? Where shall I put it?"

Annoyed, Willie called out, "Dunderweather! Put it where you got it, you fool!" Then Willie turned over to settle back to sleep.

At once the man's voice replied, "I have waited many, many years to hear those words. Now come here, and I will show you something."

At first, Willie balked because he wanted to sleep, but the voice kept insisting. Finally, Willie got up and followed the voice along a walk of large flagstones that led from the porch to the summerhouse. Flowers grew along the path. They were in full bloom.

The voice stopped in an area above one of the flagstones. The voice said to Willie, "Lift it."

Willie struggled with the stone, as it was quite heavy. Finally, he managed to lift the flagstone. Under the stone, he found a pot of gold!

"Take it. It's yours," said the mysterious voice. Then the voice disappeared.

In the morning, Willie awoke and thought that surely he had dreamed all of these events. But then, as he walked along the flagstone path, he noticed that one of the stones appeared to be out of place. Quickly, he lifted the stone and saw a large pot. He took the pot of gold to Ezra, saying, "This belongs to you."

"No, not to me," said Ezra, as he did not recognize the pot, nor the gold.

"Nor to me," said Willie. He told Ezra the story of the mysterious voice and how it had told him to lift the stone, and how, when he had lifted the stone, he had found the gold.

Sarah, who was listening closely, suggested, "Why don't you divide the money into equal parts?"

Both Ezra and Willie agreed that was a good idea. And so, each had enough money to last a lifetime.

The Dance of the Nymphs

One moonlit night, Johnny was returning home from a weary trip to a nearby town. He was helping a friend replace the roof on his barn. A big storm had blown it off the week before. Johnny felt-tired, so he decided to sit down by one of the farm buildings near his home. In a short time he was fast asleep.

After a while, Johnny awoke. At first he wasn't sure what had awakened him, but then he thought he heard the sound of soft music. He held his breath and listened quietly. Soon he heard a small voice calling, "All join hands!"

It seemed to be coming from the direction of a cornfield. Becoming increasingly curious, Johnny crept along the side of the building and looked around the corner. To his amazement, he saw beautiful maidens with their bare limbs gleaming in the moonlight. Gracefully, they began to dance in the cornfield, around and around to the sweet, soft music.

Johnny watched in awe as the beautiful maidens danced for what seemed like hours and hours. Finally, a strong desire to dance overcame Johnny. Johnny jumped out from behind the building and ran into the cornfield, right into the midst of the beautiful maidens. Johnny threw his arms around one of the dancers. To his shock, as he embraced her in his arms, she immediately turned into a cornstalk. Quickly, he reached for another beautiful maiden, only to have her, too, turn into a cornstalk. One after another, as he went to embrace each beautiful maiden in his arms, she turned into a cornstalk. He glanced at the entire field, from end to end, dismayed to see it crowded with cornstalks! Yet he knew he had heard the music, and he knew he had seen the dancing. Bewildered, Johnny stumbled down the path toward his home.

The Spirit of the Faithful Son

Once, long ago, a man who had been a good father and husband lay dying. He called his oldest son and made him promise that he would remain at home to take care of his mother and his brothers and sisters. He asked that his son always provide food and shelter for his family. The son agreed.

After the death of his father, the son did exactly as he had promised. He took care of his family, providing food and shelter as his father had asked of him. In time, this oldest son became ill. Shortly thereafter, he died.

After his burial, his spirit came to his mother at each meal time. After a while, his mother became concerned, thinking that her son had committed a serious crime, and therefore, could find no rest in the grave. One day, she said to his spirit, "Why do you come back to your home? Have you done wrong?"

"Oh, no. I promised father that I would always see that you had enough food and shelter, and I am just keeping my promise," replied the son.

The mother thanked her son and told him that he had done a good job when he was alive. He had done such a good job that she and his brothers and sisters had all that they needed, even now, after he had died. She told her son that she would call for him if they needed something.

At that, the oldest son's spirit disappeared and never came back.

The Father's Ghost

In the past, there was a very old highway that ran between Kutztown and Reading in Pennsylvania. Quite often, this highway would flood, and there was one spot in particular that became very foggy on a regular basis. Now it happened that Harry came upon this place one foggy night as he was coming home. Because of the fog, he did not realize that the spot had flooded deeper than usual. He did not have a chance to escape. Come morning, Harry was found dead.

Several years later, the Kreider family was coming home from attending services at Ebenezer country church. The night was very foggy and the family crept along in their old car at a snail's pace. Suddenly, a man appeared, carrying an old-fashioned lantern. He came toward their car on the driver's side, and then crossed over to the other side. As he passed each window, he peered in, as if to inquire, "Why did you almost hit me?" Then he continued on his way.

Scared, the family spoke to no one about the matter. After a time, others reported seeing the same man. Eventually, someone recognized him as Harry, the man who had died at that very place.

About one year later, at night, Harry's son, Ezra, was driving a bus to Reading when he saw the ghost. Ezra stopped the bus, got out, walked back to the spirit, and asked, "What do you seek? What do you want?"

The spirit answered, "Nothing, Ezra, nothing."

And that was the last time anyone saw Harry.

The Speaking Horses

Once, many, many years ago, there was a farmer named Hiram. Hiram was known throughout the county because he spoke roughly to everyone and everything, including his horses. Hiram was very harsh with his animals, making them work long hours and feeding them little food.

One year, just as Christmas was drawing near, Hiram overheard his friends and neighbors discussing some of the mysterious events that happened Christmas Eve. Hiram did not believe them to be true, even when one of his closest friends insisted, "It's true. I personally heard the horses and cattle talking just before midnight."

Hiram said, "I will not believe it to be true unless I, myself, hear the horses and cattle speaking."

Hiram decided to see (and hear) for himself. Several hours before midnight that Christmas Eve, Hiram stole into the horses stable and hid himself in a pile of straw. Just before midnight, he awoke to the sound of voices. Listening very quietly, he heard one of the horses say, "We have a very cruel master. He makes us work all day and gives us very little to eat."

A second horse replied, "We could work much more if we had more to eat. He is not as good to us as the Lord is to him."

Hearing this, Hiram became upset. He felt guilty and promised to himself that very moment to feed the horses more food. The next day, he started to give all the animals more food, and he continued to do so throughout the year. As a result, his horses worked harder, and Hiram prospered more than ever.

Big John and the Devil

Big John was a blacksmith—a very good blacksmith. One day, as he was working, a tired, hungry old man stopped by his shop. The old man was seeking food and rest. Big John offered the old man some of his lunch and invited him to sit down and rest.

Some time later, when Big John came back to check on his visitor, he was surprised to see a young man in the old man's place. The visitor introduced himself as Saint Peter.

Saint Peter said, "For your kindness, I will grant you three wishes."

Big John thought for a minute. He said, "First, whoever takes my hammer will not be able to let go of it until I set him free. Second, whoever sits in this rocking chair will not be able to get up until I set him free. Third, whoever touches this Japonica bush will become tangled within it and will not be able to get free until I set him free."

Saint Peter thought that these were silly wishes, but because Big John had asked for these things, Saint Peter granted the wishes.

Some time later, Big John and his wife were having a big argument. While they were arguing, his wife wished that he would "go with the Devil."

Shortly after this, as Big John was working in his shop, a very small devil came to visit him. The devil said, "My father sent me to bring you to him, Big John."

Big John answered, "I can't go until I finish my work. Why don't you help me finish this job."

The young devil grabbed the hammer, only to discover that he could not let go of the hammer.

"Please, let me go," begged the little devil. Finally, Big John agreed to let him go, but only if he promised never to return. Sobbing, the little devil agreed, and Big John set him free.

Several years later, Big John had another argument with his wife and, again, she wished that he would "go with the Devil."

Shortly after this, as Big John was working in his shop, a teenage devil arrived, saying, "My father sent me to bring you to him, Big John."

Big John answered, "I can't go until I finish my work. Why don't you have a seat until I am finished."

After the teenage devil had rocked awhile in the chair, he discovered that he could not get up. He begged Big John to free him. "Please, let me go! I promise that I will leave and not return."

Finally, Big John agreed and set him free.

It was many years later when Big John had yet another argument with his wife. Again, she wished that he would "go with the Devil."

Some time later, as Big John was working in his blacksmith shop, the Devil himself arrived. He demanded that Big John go with him.

Big John tried to stall the Devil, saying, "I have to finish my work. People are counting on me."

Furious, the Devil grabbed a branch from a bush by the door (the Japonica bush). Suddenly, the Devil found himself entwined and entangled within the bush. The more he struggled to free himself, the more entangled he became. He could not get free. He was furious, and he had to ask Big John to free him. Finally, after agreeing to leave Big John alone, and after agreeing never to come back, Big John set the Devil free.

After many years of good deeds, Big John died and went to Heaven. Saint Peter met him at the gate. Saint Peter checked his books. He noted the many good deeds that Big John had accomplished in his lifetime, but . . . Saint Peter also saw the record of certain deeds that were "not so good." Saint Peter refused to let Big John into Heaven and sent him below.

Well, when the Devil saw Big John coming toward him, he locked all the doors. The Devil didn't want Big John to stay with him. Big John didn't know what to do—neither place wanted him!

"What shall I do?" cried Big John.

Finally, the Devil gave him a lantern. If you watch closely at night, you might see Big John wandering through the fields with his lantern—looking for eternal rest.

Ascension Day

One year on Ascension Day, Lizzie and Katie, two girls from Jacobus, were driving their buggy along a country road. Suddenly, they noticed that the sky was becoming very dark, and that storm clouds were forming overhead. As they hurried along, both girls became very frightened by the loud claps of thunder and the bold flashes of lightning striking all around them.

Katie began to fret and worry. Looking up at the dark sky, she said, "I don't think we will make it home."

Lizzie anxiously replied, "You are not, by chance, wearing any clothes that you sewed yourself this very day, are you?"

"Why yes, I am wearing a new petticoat that I just finished this morning," Katie answered.

"Well, for heaven's sake, take it off right now and throw it away! No wonder there is lightning," shouted Lizzie.

Katie jumped off the buggy, tore off her garment at once, and put it under an old hickory tree beside the road. Quickly, Katie jumped back into the buggy and the girls drove on. They had not gone far when they saw a blinding flash of lightning and heard a terrific clap of thunder. Turning around to look, the girls saw that the lightning had split the old hickory tree from top to bottom and had torn the petticoat to shreds.

Ascension Thursday

Many, many years ago, there was an old reverend, Reverend Helfrich, who was much loved as a pastor and known throughout Lehigh county in Pennsylvania. One year, as he was driving home from a pastoral visitation on Ascension Thursday, his horse lost a shoe. Driving to a nearby blacksmith, he asked the man to shoe his horse.

The smith replied, "I would gladly shoe your horse, Reverend Helfrich, but this is Ascension Day. You know I can't do any unnecessary work today."

"Don't worry about that. This is necessary—so that I can get home," replied Reverend Helfrich.

It was known throughout the area that, for any work performed on a Sunday, or on any religious day such as Ascension Thursday, one was not to ask for payment, nor was one to offer any payment.

After the blacksmith finished shoeing the horse, the Reverend asked, "What is the cost?"

"Nothing!" cried the smith.

As he was driving away from the shop, Reverend Helfrich said, "Oh, by the way, while I was standing around, I dropped a dollar bill. Should you find it when you clean up, just keep it."

When the blacksmith returned to his shop, he found the dollar bill lying on the floor.

The Way to Peel an Apple

Once there was a young girl named Hattie. Hattie had three suitors, and she was quite perplexed—she could not decide which one to choose for a husband. Finally, her mother told her to invite each one to see her, separately, and to give each one an apple to eat, and a knife with which to peel it.

Hattie first invited Henry, and when he arrived, she offered him an apple and a knife. Henry took the apple and ate it to the core, without peeling it. When Hattie told her mother, her mother just shook her head and said, "Henry will not make a good husband. He does not care what he eats or how he eats it."

Samuel was the second gentleman that Hattie invited. Hattie offered him an apple and a knife. Samuel peeled the apple very thinly and ate it, carefully, to the core. Well, when Hattie told her mother this, she shook her head again and said, "Samuel will not make a good husband, either. He takes everything he can get."

Finally, Hattie invited Jake. When Hattie offered Jake an apple and a knife, he peeled it thickly, and then ate only part of the apple. When Hattie told her mother, she said, "This man will make a good husband. He peeled the apple thickly, knowing that we would throw the leavings to the chickens, and they, too, would have something to eat. He is the one that you should choose!"

The Best of Three

Once, a long time ago, when Solly was a young man, he told his mother that he would like to marry, but he feared that he did not know how to choose a good wife. His mother said to him, "Saddle your horse and ride to the home of the girl that you have in mind. When you are close to her home, dismount and tie your horse to a tree. Then, go toward the house. When you see the girl, tell her that your horse suddenly became ill. Ask her for some scrapings from the kneading trough."

Solly did just this. He rode until he came close to the home of Emma, a girl he knew fairly well. He dismounted, tied his horse to a tree, and walked toward the house. When he saw Emma on the porch, he said, "My horse has suddenly become ill with the colic." He asked, "Would you please give me a handful of the scrapings from the kneading trough so that I may feed him?"

Emma answered, "Scrapings I shall gladly give you," and she went into the house. Shortly, she returned with two heaping handfuls, saying, "If this is not enough, I can get more."

Solly thanked her and left. He returned to his mother and told her what had happened, but she shook her head and said, "Try again."

The next day, Solly rode out again. This time he stopped at Anna's house. To his request, Anna replied, "When we are baking, we clean our kneading trough, so there are no scrapings to be had."

When Solly told his mother this, she sadly shook her head and said, "Try again, Solly."

This time, when Solly rode out, he headed toward the home of a girl whom he had heard about, but had never met—Grace. Again, he requested scrapings from the kneading trough for his sick horse. Grace answered, "I don't know whether I can get any scrapings, but I will try."

After a short time, Grace returned with a small handful. As she gave Solly the scrapings, she said, apologetically, "This is all

I could get from the corners of the trough. I am sorry I cannot give you more."

Solly thanked her and rode home. When he told his mother about Grace, she smiled and said, "Grace is the one for you. Seek no further."

The Farmer's Horses

There was once a successful farmer named Samuel who had a serious problem with his horses. One day, after a hard day's work in the fields, the horses refused to enter the barn.

No matter what Samuel did, the horses refused to cross through the doorway and enter the barn. First he coaxed them, then he tempted them with carrots, and then he removed their harnesses. Finally, in desperation, he snapped a whip. At this, the horses entered the barn.

The next day, when Samuel returned from the fields, the horses again refused to enter the barn. Once again, Samuel coaxed and tempted the horses, but they would not enter the barn until he snapped the whip.

Deeply disturbed by his horses' behavior, Samuel walked to the village to see a braucher. After hearing the farmer's story, the braucher advised, "Wait until the next time the horses refuse to cross through the doorway. Then, slowly pound a sixteen- or twenty-penny nail into the sill."

Samuel thought this was strange—and useless—advice. He muttered to himself all the way home. He didn't understand how the braucher's solution could possibly affect his horses.

Several days later, after another hard day's work in the fields, Samuel led his horses to the barn. They refused to enter. Again, Samuel coaxed and tempted them, but still they refused to enter the barn.

Remembering what the braucher had said, Samuel hammered a nail into the sill of the doorway, to a depth between one-third and one-half of its length. No sooner had Samuel done this, an old woman, who was walking down the road by his barn, pleaded to him, "Please, draw out that nail or I shall die!"

"Will you leave my horses alone?" asked the farmer.

"Yes, yes!" cried the old woman.

Samuel drew out the nail and the woman disappeared. She was never seen again.

And . . . the horses never again balked at entering the barn.

Counting Noses

Many years ago, a group of thirteen men were traveling through the countryside. They came to a stream of water and decided to rest for awhile. The men stretched on the lawn, drank from the stream, and explored on foot the area around the stream.

After an hour, they decided it was time to move on. But one of the men thought that someone was missing. They argued among themselves, until the leader suggested they count to see if they were all present.

The first one counting said, "If I am I, you are one, you are two, you are three. . ." and so on until the last one was twelve.

"There are only twelve of us," said the one who was counting.

"That's wrong," said another. "Let me count. I am I, you are one, you are two," and so on to the last who was twelve.

A third man counted and arrived at the same results. He insisted that one was missing.

They could not agree and began to argue. Another traveler came along and asked, "What is the problem?"

They all started to answer at once. Finally, the leader said, "We were thirteen men traveling together and now we think one is missing. When we count, we get only twelve. Tell us, are we twelve or thirteen men?"

The traveler shook his head and refused to answer. Instead, he suggested, "Why don't you put your noses in that soft mud by the river bank, then count the holes?" With that, he rode away.

The group decided to try the traveler's suggestion, so they all went over to the river bank. One by one they leaned over and pressed their nose into the mud. When they counted the holes, they found that thirteen were present.

"I sort of thought that we all were here," muttered one as they continued on their way.

Geneova

Many years ago, a beautiful young woman named Geneova was married to a handsome prince. They were extremely happy together.

This prince had many servants, and among them was one who was very mean and jealous of Geneova. He wanted to entice Geneova into sin, and tempted her often. But she was so happy with the Prince that she never yielded to his temptations or evil tricks. This made the servant quite angry, and he began to hate Geneova. He told the Prince that his beautiful Geneova had been unfaithful and deceitful.

The servant was so convincing that the Prince believed him. He was so furious that he drove Geneova and her new son from the castle and into the forest. He demanded that his soldiers kill her and the baby and bring her tongue to him as proof that she was dead.

Geneova begged and pleaded with the soldiers to let them live. After all, the young boy needed a mother to nurse him and help him grow. Now the soldiers were very fond of Geneova, and they could not understand why the Prince had turned against her. After some consultation, the soldiers agreed to set her free if she promised to live deep in the forest. Geneova agreed, and taking her baby, walked into the dark forest, not knowing where to go since there were no paths or homes. The soldiers then killed a doe, and carried the tongue home to the Prince.

Meanwhile, Geneova walked through the dark forest until she came to a large cliff. Climbing the cliff, she discovered a bear's den. Exhausted, she entered the cave, and putting her baby down, fell asleep. When she awoke, she decided the cave would make a good shelter, and there she made her home. She lived on berries, herbs, bark, and roots. Every day a doe came to the cliff and Geneova was able to get milk for her baby. Thus she lived many, many years.

Geneova's son grew into a fine young man, learning the ways of the forest. He hunted for food and clothing for both of them. And he listened to stories his mother told about life in the palace. She told him often that she had been falsely accused by the servant and had been unjustly driven from the palace.

One day, Geneova gave the young man a ring that had been given to her by her father on the day she was married. The ring had the family crest upon it. The boy was determined that when he grew up, he would go to his father to defend his mother and accuse the servant for his treachery.

It wasn't long until this boy was grown. He left on his journey to find the palace. Coming to the edge of the forest, he saw the palace in the distance.

At the end of the day, he came to the palace and demanded to see the Prince. At first, he was refused entrance, but then one of the soldiers, who happened to be Geneova's brother, spotted the ring with the family crest. Recognizing the ring as one his father had given to his sister, he went to the Prince and requested that he see the young man.

The Prince agreed, and when the young man was brought face to face with him, he listened intently to his story. The Prince demanded that the evil servant be brought into the large hall.

When the servant arrived, seeing the young man before the Prince, he confessed to the evil he had done. The Prince ordered the servant held, and left immediately to go into the forest to look for Geneova. With horses and the young man to guide him, they arrived at the cave when the moon was high in the sky. The Prince brought Geneova back to the palace, where she lived happily with him for the rest of her life.

As for the servant, the Prince ordered him tied to four oxen, one limb to each ox. Then, striking the oxen, he watched them race off to the four winds.

Pennsylvania Dutchmen Always Give Testimony

A long time ago, there lived a farmer named Jake, and his daughter, Rebecca. These two were hard-working and religious individuals. They often went to church to give testimony to God. One particular Wednesday, after a very long day in the tobacco fields, Jake came into the house saying, "I want to go to Prayer Meeting tonight, but I am so tired and sticky and dirty from all this heat. I don't think we have enough time to get ready and get there."

"Oh, why don't you just wash your face and feet? That will get rid of some of the dirt. Don't worry about changing your clothes. We can take the shortcut through the woods," suggested Rebecca.

"I don't think the shortcut is a good idea. There are bears in those woods," said Jake.

But he really wanted to go to Prayer Meeting, so they did as Rebecca suggested. In a few minutes, they hurried off together on the path through the woods, heading to Prayer Meeting. Jake led the way. Over halfway through the woods, Jake rounded a bend in the path and came face to face with a huge brown bear! The bear reached out, grabbed Jake, giving him a big, big hug! Jake struggled to get free, but the bear just played with him, tearing his shirt and mauling him.

"Dear God, help me," cried Jake.

After a while, the bear became bored, spotted something else moving in the woods, and dropped Jake.

Rebecca helped her father to his feet, and they continued on their way to church. Even though they were late, they decided to slip in and sit in the back row and just listen. Jake did not want anyone to see his torn shirt and his dirty face. However, the preacher saw Jake and called upon him to give testimony. Jake, clutching his torn shirt, stood and declared, "God is good, giving us many things. He gives us all that we have—but, he is not very good in a bear fight!"

The Great Need

Years ago, it was the custom of many folks to save for "Die Gross Nod," an old dialectal expression for famine, or perhaps hard times in the future. It was in these olden days that Ezra and his wife, Katie, lived on a farm in the back country. Often Ezra would say, "Katie, we really must save for Die Gross Nod, the time when the great need comes."

One day, when Ezra was in the fields working and Katie was alone doing her housework, there was a knock at the door. Katie opened the door and, not recognizing the person asked, "Who are you?"

"I am Mr. Need," the stranger replied.

"Are you the one they call "The Great Need?" asked Katie.

"Well, yes, I guess I am," the stranger replied.

"Oh, my husband and I have been waiting a long time for you," cried Katie.

"Come in while I gather all the money we've been saving for you. Would you like a piece of pie while you wait?"

Mr. Need sat in the kitchen eating his pie, while Katie gathered their savings from the various hiding places in their home. When she had found all the money, she gave it to Mr. Need. Then, Mr. Need took his leave, marveling at how generous she had been.

When Ezra returned home from work, Katie was so excited she could hardly speak. "Mr. Need was here today. I gave him all that we had saved for him. He was really surprised!" said Katie.

After Ezra recovered from the shock of losing all their savings, he cried, "Dummkopp! You are so stupid! I do not care to stay with one so stupid. I am leaving and won't be back unless I meet someone more stupid than you!"

Ezra left that very day. He traveled many miles and finally came to a barn where several men were working very hard. He watched them for some time, then said, "What are you doing?"

"We are trying to put the white horse in the hayloft for 'en neschtoi,' that is, a nest egg." Now, it was the custom when gathering eggs, one was always left in the nest to encourage the hens to lay more eggs. These men believed that putting the white horse in the hayloft would encourage an imaginary animal to lay a colt.

"Dummkopp!" said Ezra, "They are stupid, but not as stupid as my Katie."

And so he continued walking. Eventually he climbed a high hill. Spotting a hut down in the valley, he walked down the hill until he came to the hut. The windows were open and inside sat a little old woman. When she saw Ezra, she invited him in. "Where do you come from?" she asked.

"Vun owwe runner," replied Ezra. Now this phrase had two meanings. One meant coming down from a hill to a valley, while the other meant to come down from heaven.

"Oh, I am so glad to see you!" exclaimed the old woman. "Tell me, how is my son, Michael, getting along up there?"

"Not so well," answered Ezra, "He has no money, no shoes, and no food."

"Oh my," said the woman as she got up. "I am so happy that someone has come so that I can send some things to my Michael."

She gathered food and clothes and all the money she could find. She gave all these things to Ezra and told him to take them to Michael. Ezra just shook his head. He had finally met one who was more stupid than his wife, Katie. He hurried home to Katie, and lived happily with her for many years.

Chapter 14

Eileschpiggel

Every culture has a trickster in their folk stories. Eileschpiggel (pronounced I-la-sh-pe-gull, which is Pennsylvania Dutch for "Owl Mirror") is a trickster character among the folktales of the Pennsylvania Germans. In these tales he is held in great affection because of his lovable and cunning nature, unlike the European stories about him in which his tricks are generally more brutal and malicious.

The Swimming Contest

Eileschpiggel and the Devil were always having loud boasting sessions, about anything and everything. Each one would try to outdo the other. One day, they were boasting about their ability to swim great distances. Finally, to settle the matter, they agreed to a swimming contest in the great Susquehanna River.

On the appointed day and at the appointed time, the Devil and Eileschpiggel met at the river. A large crowd had gathered to watch the contest. Now the Devil was ready for this contest. He had been practicing each and every day since they had made the wager.But Eileschpiggel had not practiced at all, and he was definitely not ready.

Eileschpiggel said, "Before we start, a calf must be butchered and roasted."

"Whatever for?" asked the Devil.

"Well, I am not going to swim for fourteen days without eating," answered Eileschpiggel.

When the Devil heard that, he threw up his hands and fled.

Some time later, the Devil returned and began boasting about his strength. It wasn't very long until Eileschpiggel and the Devil were boasting as to which had more strength.

The Devil said, "I can lift that horse."

Eileschpiggel laughed and said, "That's nothing, I can lift the wagon *and* the horse."

The arguing continued until, finally, the Devil walked over to a huge oak tree and pulled it up by its roots and threw it into the air. Eileschpiggel just hooted. And so the Devil demanded, "Show me your strength or be quiet."

Eileschpiggel thought for a minute and then began to climb a huge tree. Immediately, the Devil became curious and asked, "What are you doing? Why are you climbing the tree?"

Eileschpiggel replied, "I don't want to waste time in pulling up one tree. I am going to bind the tops of several trees so I can pull them all up at once."

With that, the Devil again gave up the contest and fled.

The Sewing Contest

Once, when Eileschpiggel was working as a tailor, a man came to him to order a suit. As Eileschpiggel was sewing on the suit, the Devil happened by. It wasn't very long before the two began boasting.

"I can sew faster than you!" said the Devil.

"You cannot!" cried Eileschpiggel.

Before long, the two made a wager as to which one could sew a pair of pantaloons the fastest. While the Devil was threading the needles, Eileschpiggel said, "Don't make my thread too short."

"I won't," answered the Devil. The Devil thought, "if Eileschpiggel asks for a long thread, that must mean he can sew faster with longer thread. Mine must be longer." The Devil cut the thread for his needle twice as long as the one he cut for Eileschpiggel.

Then, because the Devil did not want to be seen, they both crawled into a bakeoven to sew for the contest. They both began sewing. Eileschpiggel had no problem because of the shorter thread, but the Devil discovered that every time he wanted to draw out the thread, he had to crawl out of the oven.

"This isn't working," said the Devil. "We will have to move the contest to the housetop."

After they had climbed onto the roof, they once again began sewing. This time, the Devil discovered that his thread was so long that it became tangled around the chimney and the eaves of the house. Every time he wanted to draw out the thread, the Devil had to stop to free his thread. Meanwhile, Eileschpiggel kept on sewing. The Devil said, disgustedly, "It's no use; I can't keep up with you!" Then he fled.

Farming on Shares

One year, the Devil and Eileschpiggel made a pact to farm on shares. For the first year, the Devil claimed, "My share will be that part of the crop that grows above the ground, and you, Eileschpiggel, can have the part of the crop that grows under the ground."

Eileschpiggel thought for a minute, and agreed. That year, he planted turnips. Eileschpiggel worked hard all during the planting season to ensure that he would have a good crop, but the Devil did nothing.

When it came time to harvest the crops, the Devil appeared. He said, "I've come to claim my share."

Eileschpiggel smiled and said, "Fine. As I recall, I am to have the roots, while you, the Devil, get the leaves."

The second year, before planting began, the Devil came again and demanded, "This year, I want whatever grows under the ground as my share, and you can have whatever grows above the ground."

Eileschpiggel thought for a while, then agreed. That year, he planted wheat. He worked hard all during the planting and growing season, but the Devil was nowhere to be seen. When harvest time arrived, so did the Devil. The Devil declared, "I've come for my shares. Remember, my share is whatever grows underground."

When they divided the crops, the Devil got the roots and Eileschpiggel got the grain.

The third year, the Devil appeared again, hoping to outdo Eileschpiggel. He claimed, "This year, I will have the rights to both the tops and the roots of the crop. You, Eileschpiggel, can have whatever is in the middle."

Now, Eileschpiggel gave much thought to what he would plant that year. Finally, he agreed to the Devil's condition. And, once more, Eileschpiggel worked very hard during the planting and growing season, so that he would have a good crop when harvest time came. Finally, the Devil appeared to make his claim.

Eileschpiggel said, "Let's see, you claimed the rights to both the tops and the roots, while I get the middle. Because I planted corn this year, that leaves you with the tassels and the roots, while I get the corn itself!"

Eileschpiggel had tricked him again! The Devil became so enraged that he disappeared and didn't bother farmer Eileschpiggel for a very long time.

Logic Is Logic

One day, Eileschpiggel decided that he needed some wood, so he drove his team of horses to town. When he arrived at the local country store, he started to load the wood onto his wagon, one piece at a time. As people passed by, they heard him say, "If the horses can pull this piece of wood, surely they can pull *this* piece of wood."

Reasoning in this manner, he continued to load the wood onto the wagon until it was completely full. Only then did he discover that the load was too heavy for the horses to pull. He began to unload the wood, one piece at a time. As he unloaded each successive piece, he muttered to himself, "If the horses can't pull this piece of wood, surely they can't pull *this* piece of wood."

He continued unloading until the wagon was empty. Then he drove home without any wood at all.

Eileschpiggel, the Farmhand

Once, Eileschpiggel worked as a farmhand. One day, the farmer Moses directed Eileschpiggel to hitch up a four-horse team.

"Hitch the sorrels in front and the two black horses in the back, then bring the team out into the field where I will be working," said Moses.

After a long time, Eileschpiggel had not appeared. Moses became impatient. He went to see what was keeping Eileschpiggel. When he got to the barn, he couldn't believe his eyes! Eileschpiggel had hitched the sorrels to the front of the wagon, the black horses to the rear of the wagon.

"What does this mean?" cried Moses. "Did I not tell you to hitch the sorrels in the front, and the blacks behind?"

"That's exactly what I have done. The sorrels are in front and the blacks are behind. And, with a hitching such as this, the Devil himself can't do any driving," said Eileschpiggel.

"Get out and go tie up the sheaves," said Moses disgustedly. Now Moses used the word *uffbinne*, which means "to tie up," but it also has the meaning "to untie," and this was what Eileschpiggel thought Moses had meant. Eileschpiggel went out into the field and began untying all the sheaves of wheat that Moses had bound.

When Moses returned to the field, he saw something that dismayed him. "What have you done?" he cried.

"I have untied the sheaves, just as you commanded," replied Eileschpiggel.

Moses just shook his head in disbelief.

Soon after, Moses decided to give Eileschpiggel another chance. He directed Eileschpiggel to grease the heavy farm wagon.

"Grease it well—we will use it to haul stones from the field to fill up that mudhole," said Moses.

Eileschpiggel took the big can of grease and started to work. After some time, he came to his master and said that he couldn't finish the job, as he had run out of grease.

"Impossible!" shouted Moses. "There was enough grease there to do three wagons! I must see what you have done!"

He quickly went out to look at the wagon and discovered that Eileschpiggel had been smearing grease over the body of the wagon.

"What have you done? That isn't greasing," cried Moses.

"You told me to grease the wagon and that is just what I have done," said Eileschpiggel.

"To grease a wagon means that you put grease here and here," cried Moses as he pointed to the spindles.

"That's not greasing the wagon, that is greasing the spindles," said Eileschpiggel.

Soon after, Moses sent Eileschpiggel to pick peas in a field that lay a good distance away. Surely he can do this right, thought the farmer.

"After you pick the peas, hull them on the field and then you will be able to carry them all home at once," said Moses.

Eileschpiggel obeyed the farmer. He picked all the peas and hulled them on the field. Then he put them into a large sack and started home.

Now, there was a small hole in the bottom of the sack, and it wasn't long before Eileschpiggel noticed that some of the peas had fallen through the hole and were rolling down the hill in front of him.

"If you prefer to go that way," said Eileschpiggel, "then that way you shall go." He emptied the bag and placed all the peas on the side of the hill. Then he went home.

"But, where are the peas?" cried Moses when he saw that Eileschpiggel was empty-handed.

"Oh, they're coming, maybe a little too slowly, but they are coming," answered Eileschpiggel. "I carried them uphill; downhill they need no help."

The Devil Does Not Recognize His Favorite Implement

At one time, Eileschpiggel was working as a blacksmith. Earlier on, Eileschpiggel had made a deal with the Devil to sell his soul. One day, as Eileschpiggel was very busy at the anvil, the Devil appeared.

"Eileschpiggel," said the Devil, "your time is up. I have come to fetch you. Come along now."

"I am much too busy to go with you today," said Eileschpiggel. "I am a good blacksmith, and I have much work to complete. I can't go with you. I can't leave my work unfinished."

They argued at great length, and finally agreed that the Devil would go away for a short time. When he came back, Eileschpiggel would go with him immediately, but only if the Devil could guess what tool Eileschpiggel was making. If he could not guess correctly, then Eileschpiggel was free forever from the power of the Devil.

So the Devil went away. When he returned, he found Eileschpiggel working on a piece of iron. It appeared that he was molding the iron into a pitchfork with two tines. Eileschpiggel had turned one tine slightly upward, but had bent the other tine upward at nearly a right angle.

"What am I making?" asked Eileschpiggel.

"Oh, that's easy," said the Devil. "A hayfork."

"Wrong," said Eileschpiggel as he turned the piece of iron over so the tines were pointing downward. He pounded the straight tine in line with the other.

"This is a manure hook," said Eileschpiggel. "Your favorite tool for torture." With that, the Devil knew that he had lost the wager, and he disappeared forever.

Eileschpiggel and the Cattle

Once Eileschpiggel was annoying his neighbors with tricks of one kind or another. When he would boast and brag about his feats, making himself so obnoxious, his neighbors started talking about him behind his back. They soon began to plot together on how they could rid themselves of him once and for all.

One day, the neighbors waited for Eileschpiggel to come down the path toward the village. It wasn't long before they saw him rounding the bend, and they rushed over, grabbed him, and shoved him into a cask they had ready. After sealing the lid, they began to roll the cask toward the sea.

On their way to the sea, they came upon a tavern, and since it was a hot day, they thought about how nice a cool drink would be. Leaving the cask outside, they entered the tavern to drink to the success of ridding themselves of Eileschpiggel.

While they were in the tavern a drover came along with a large herd of cattle. Eileschpiggel heard them coming, and he began to moan, "I cannot do it, and I will not do it. I cannot do it, and I will not do it."

The drover stopped, looked around, and listened. He didn't see anyone, yet he heard someone say, "I cannot do it, and I will not do it. I cannot do it, and I will not do it."

The drover realized the voice was coming from the cask, so he walked over and said, "What can't you do?"

"They want me to marry the King's daughter, and I don't want to. They are taking me to the King in this cask to make me marry her—but I cannot do it! I won't do it!"

"I will! Let me marry the King's daughter!" begged the drover.

"Are you sure?" asked Eileschpiggel.

"Yes! Yes!" cried the drover.

Quickly he removed the lid to the cask and helped Eileschpiggel out. Then the drover crawled into the cask, and Eileschpiggel replaced the lid. Next, Eileschpiggel took the cattle and herded them to his house.

After a short time, his neighbors came out from the tavern and continued to roll the cask toward the sea. When they came to the bank, they pushed the cask into the water and watched it sink.

Satisfied that they had finally rid themselves of the pesky, obnoxious Eileschpiggel, they started home. They were in high spirits and quite boisterous, all talking at once about how Eileschpiggel had finally gotten what he deserved. You can imagine their surprise when they rounded the last bend in the road, near Eileschpiggel's home. There sat Eileschpiggel—and with a herd of cattle!

"How did you get here? Where did they come from? How did you get such beautiful animals?" the neighbors demanded.

"Why, at the bottom of the sea," replied Eileschpiggel. "There are many more down there. These are all that I could drive up the banks and out onto the shore to bring home. There are many more down there."

With that news, the neighbors turned and rushed back to the sea, eager to get some of those animals for themselves. When they reached the sea, they jumped in and all were drowned.

Hans Herr House. The 1719 Hans Herr House is the oldest building in Lancaster County, Pennsylvania. It was built by Christian Herr, a Swiss-German Mennonite and is a fine example of medieval Germanic architecture. It is located in Willow Street, Pennsylvania. (Photograph by Carol E. Leaman)

Detail, Pennsylvania Quilt, c.1860. Rose of Sharon Pattern. (Courtesy of The Schaeffer Collection from the Permanent Collection of Franklin and Marshall College, Lancaster, Pennsylvania, The Leonard and Mildred Rothman Gallery)

Photographs

Breaking Flax (a process involved in the making of linen). This step, breaking flax, was typically a male job. (Courtesy of the Landis Valley Museum, operated by the Pennsylvania Historical and Museum Commission)

Making Splint Oak Baskets on a Schnitzel-bank. (Courtesy of Landis Valley Museum, operated by the Pennsylvania Historical and Museum Commission)

Mary Nissly Sampler (linen with cotton and silk embroidery). (Courtesy of The Hostetter Collection from the Permanent Collection of Franklin and Marshall College, Lancaster, Pennsylvania, The Leonard and Mildred Rothman Gallery)

Stiegel-type Glass. (Courtesy of The Hostetter Collection from the Permanent Collection of Franklin and Marshall College, Pennsylvania, The Leonard and Mildred Rothman Gallery)

Redware. Made for Molly Dorat by Vickers of Chester County (1802). (Courtesy of The Hostetter Collection from the Permanent Collection of Franklin and Marshall College, Lancaster, Pennsylvania, The Leonard and Mildred Rothman Gallery)

Late 19th-century Pennsylvania Folk Art Drawing. (Courtesy of The Schaeffer Collection from the Permanent Collection of Franklin and Marshall College, Lancaster, Pennsylvania, The Leonard and Mildred Rothman Gallery)

"Winter Scene" (watercolor). Hattie Brunner (1961). (Courtesy the Permanent Collection of Franklin and Marshall College, Lancaster, Pennsylvania, The Leonard and Mildred Ruthman Gallery)

Scherenschnitte. Late 19th-century Pennsylvania German papercutting. (Courtesy of the Unger-Bassler Collection from the Permanent Collection of Franklin and Marshall College, Lancaster, Pennsylvania, The Leonard and Mildred Rothman Gallery)

Bride's Box. Continental folk art adopted by the Pennsylvania Germans. (Courtesy of The Schaeffer Collection from the Permanent Collection of Franklin and Marshall College, Lancaster, Pennsylvania, The Leonard and Mildred Rothman Gallery)

Pennsylvania Walnut Tall Case Clock. John Fisher, Yorktown (now York), c.1765. (Courtesy of the Permanent Collection of Franklin and Marshall College, Lancaster, Pennsylvania, The Leonard and Mildred Rothman Gallery)

Watercolor Drawing (artist unknown). Lake 19th-century. (Courtesy of the Unger-Bassler Collection from the Permanent Collection of Franklin and Marshall College, Lancaster, Pennsylvania)

Geburts und Taufshein (birth, baptismal, and confirmation record) for Abraham Kramer (1776), Barton and Jungmann, Reading printers, decoration attributed to Friedrich Krebs (probably Bucks County).(Courtesy of the Unger-Bassler Collection from the Permanent Collection of Franklin and Marshall College, Lancaster, Pennsylvania, The Leonard and Mildred Rothman Gallery)

Vorschrift (1842) (middle 19th-century). Indicates assimilation of the symbols/essence of the United States: decorative use of the American eagle and the motto, "E Pluribus Unum," exploring the mixing of patriotic symbolism with the language of devotional piety. (Courtesy of The Hostetter Collection from the Permanent Collection of Franklin and Marshall College, Lancaster, Pennsylvania, The Leonard and Mildred Rothman Gallery)

Part III

Recipes

Chapter 15

Favorite Pennsylvania German Recipes

Pies

Pennsylvania Dutch Pie Crust
(Makes crust for 3 pies.)

3 cups flour
pinch of salt
1 cup shortening (lard)
water

Mix shortening into the flour until crumbly. Add salt. Add water, a few drops at a time, until it is the proper consistency to roll out.

Hint: When making a fruit pie, put lower crust in a 325 degree oven for 5 minutes while you roll out the top crust. Be sure to prick the crust all over so it will lay flat when baked. This will prevent the bottom crust from becoming soggy during baking.

Apple Pie

6 large tart apples, sliced
1 tsp. cinnamon
1/8 tsp. salt
1 cup sugar

1/2 tsp. nutmeg
1 tsp. lemon juice
1 tbsp. butter

Line pie pan with pie crust dough. Bake in a 325 degree oven for 5 minutes. Fill baked crust with sliced apples. Mix sugar, spices, salt, and lemon juice. Sprinkle over apples. Dot with butter. Moisten edge of pie crust with water. Place top crust over apples, and seal edge. Cut 4 slits in the top crust for the steam to escape. Bake at 425 degrees for 50 minutes.

Schnitz Pie

1 lb. schnitz (dried apple slices)
butter
sugar

cinnamon
lemon rind or juice

Cover the dried apples with water. Soak overnight. Add water, a little lemon peel or juice, and cook until soft. Press through a colander. Stir in sugar and cinnamon to taste. Pour mixture into a pastry-lined pie pan. Dot with butter. Cover with top crust or lattice strips. Place in 425 degree oven for 15 minutes, then reduce heat to 350 degrees and bake 30 minutes.

Shoo-Fly Pie

Crumb ingredients:
1/4 cup shortening
1 cup brown sugar
1-1/2 cups flour

Mix all crumb ingredients and set aside.

Liquid ingredients:
1/4 tsp. baking soda
1/8 tsp. nutmeg
pinch of ginger
pinch of cinnamon

pinch of cloves
1/4 tsp. salt
3/4 cup molasses
3/4 cup hot water

Mix 6 dry ingredients above. Add molasses and water. Mix well.
To assemble: Beginning and ending on top of pie with crumbs, combine crumbs and liquid in alternate layers in a pie shell. Bake at 450 degrees for 15 minutes. Reduce heat to 350 degrees and bake 20 minutes.

Cookies and Cakes

Springerle
(Makes approx. 4 dozen cookies.)

4 eggs
1/2 cup powdered confectioners' sugar
1/2 to 3/4 tsp. anise extract, or 1/4 tsp. anise oil
4 cups flour

Beat eggs on high speed for 5 minutes. Add powdered sugar and beat steadily 1/2 hour. Add anise extract and flour. Mix thoroughly. Dough should be of a consistency to roll into a sheet about 1/2-inch thick. If it is not, gradually add more flour until it is the proper consistency.

Roll dough out on a floured surface or on wax paper. Cut out cookies with aluminum molds, or use wooden molds or a rolling pin with stenciled patterns. Press deeply to make a good impression.

Place cookies on wax paper and let stand in a cool place several hours, preferably overnight.

Transfer to greased, floured cookie sheet and bake at 375 degrees about 15 minutes, or until the color of straw.

Anise is a strong licorice flavor. You may wish to use the smaller amount of extract or oil.

Sugar Cakes

2 cups sugar
3/4 cup butter (use shortening or
   lard if preferred)
3 eggs
1 cup milk
4-1/2 cups flour

2 tsp. baking powder
1 tsp. baking soda
pinch of salt
vanilla flavoring to taste

Mix all ingredients. Drop onto a greased cookie sheet and bake at 325 degrees for approximately 15 minutes. These cookies will have a cake-like consistency.

Sand Tarts

Dough ingredients:
2 cups sugar
1 cup butter
4 eggs (2 will be used to brush tops of tarts)
3 cups flour

Topping ingredients:
sugar
cinnamon
nuts, chopped

Mix butter and 2 cups sugar together. Add 2 eggs and beat until creamy. Add enough flour to make a very stiff dough. Chill. Roll dough out thin. Use cookie cutters to make shapes or cut into small squares. Brush tops with remaining 2 eggs (beaten). Sprinkle with sugar, cinnamon, and chopped nuts. Bake at 300-325 degrees for 10 to 15 minutes. Watch closely.

Crumb Cake
(This is a favorite at breakfast time!)

3 cups flour
2 cups sugar
1 stick butter (1/2 cup) plus
    1 tsp. for finished cake
1 cup buttermilk

1 tsp. baking soda mixed in milk
2 eggs, separated
cinnamon

      Crumble first 3 ingredients together. Reserve 1/2 cup to be scattered over top of cake.
      Beat the egg yolks well. To the remainder of the crumbs, add the egg yolks and the buttermilk. Beat the egg whites until stiff. Fold into the cake mixture. Place mixture in a well-greased 8- or 9-inch round or square cake pan. Sprinkle 1/2 cup of crumbs over the top of the cake and bake at 375 degrees for about 45 minutes. When baked, sprinkle 1 tsp. of melted butter over the cake and dust with cinnamon.

Meat Dishes

Scrapple

1/2 lb. chopped raw meat (beef,
    pork, or liver)
1-1/4 tsp. salt
1/8 tsp. pepper
1 cup cornmeal

1 medium onion, chopped
1-1/4 qts. water
2 tsp. shortening (lard)
mold (e.g., a loaf pan)

      Brown onion slowly in 2 tsp. shortening. Add meat, salt and pepper, and water. Bring to boil and simmer for 20 minutes. Add cornmeal and boil 1 hour. Pour into dishes to mold (e.g., a loaf pan) and cool. When cold, cut into 1/4-inch slices. Fry in shortening until brown and crusty on both sides. Serve with gravy or tomato sauce.

Speck un Kraut
(Pork and Sauerkraut)

2-3 lbs. fresh pork loin
1 qt. sauerkraut, canned or fresh
water
salt and pepper

      Place pork in a large pot. Cover with cold water and cook over medium heat for 1 hour. Add sauerkraut, making sure there is enough liquid in the pan to cover all ingredients. Cook on low or simmer for 1 hour. Season to taste. Serve with mashed or boiled potatoes. Some people prefer to roast the pork and cook the sauerkraut separately.

Schnitz un Knepp
(Dried Apple Slices and Dumplings)

1-1/2 to 3 pounds cured ham
1 qt. dried apples
2 cups flour
1 egg
4 tsp. baking powder

3 tbsp. shortening, melted
1/4 tsp. pepper
1 tbsp. milk
1 tsp. salt

Boil ham for 2 hours. Clean dried apples. Cover apples with water and soak while ham is cooking. When meat is cooked, add apples and the water they soaked in to the ham pot. Boil for 1 hour.

Dumpling (knepp) batter: Sift the dry ingredients together. Beat egg. Add egg, melted shortening, and milk to the dry ingredients. Drop batter by spoonfuls into the boiling liquid of the ham and apples. Cover tightly and cook for 15 minutes. Some enjoy making this recipe without the ham.

Chicken Pot Pie

1 cup flour
1 egg
2 tsp. baking powder
1/2 eggshell of water
small tsp. salt

4 lb. chicken (cooked)
2 tbsp. minced parsley
4 medium-sized potatoes
water to cover

Mix the first 5 ingredients. Roll out on floured surface or wax paper. Cut into 2-inch squares. Dice cooked chicken. Pare and quarter potatoes. Cover dough squares, chicken, potatoes, and parsley with boiling water. Cook approximately 2 hours on top of stove.

Salads

Dandelion Salad with Hot Bacon Dressing

dandelion greens
4 thick slices bacon
1/2 cup whipping cream
1 tbsp. butter
2 eggs, beaten

1 tsp. salt
4 tbsp. vinegar
1 tbsp. sugar
pinch of black pepper

Wash dandelion greens and pat dry. Place in salad bowl and set aside. Cut bacon into small cubes. Fry quickly until crisp and pour over dandelion greens. Melt butter and whipping cream in skillet over low heat. Beat eggs. Add eggs, salt, pepper, sugar, and vinegar to the warm cream mixture. Cook over high heat until dressing is thick. Pour hot dressing over the dandelion greens. Stir well and serve immediately.

Cucumber Salad

1 medium cucumber
1 medium onion
1/4 cup vinegar
1/2 cup water

1/2 tbsp. salt
1/4 cup milk
2 tbsp. sugar

Pare and thinly slice cucumber and onion. Mix all other ingredients and pour over cucumbers and onion slices. Let stand 1 hour or longer before serving.

Soup

Chicken Corn Soup

Soup ingredients:

1 stewing chicken (approx. 3-4 lbs.)
4 qts. water
1 onion, chopped
10 ears sweet corn

1/2 cup celery, chopped with leaves
2 hard-boiled eggs, chopped
salt and pepper
rivels

Rivels ingredients:

1 cup flour
pinch salt
1 egg
milk

Cut up chicken and slice onion. Place chicken and onion in water and cook slowly until tender, strain broth, but do not discard. Add salt. Cut the chicken into 1-inch pieces and return to broth. Add corn (cut from the cob), celery, and seasonings. Boil together until corn is soft.

Rivels: Combine flour, salt, egg, and a little milk. Mixture should be firm enough to hold together. Rub dough through hands and let shreds (rivels) drop into the hot soup. Add chopped eggs. Boil slowly for 15 minutes.

Pretzel Soup

2 lbs. butter pretzels
4 cups milk
2 cups water

3 tbsp. butter
salt and pepper
parsley, chopped

Blend butter and flour and set aside. Combine milk and water and cook over medium heat. Stir butter/flour mixture into milk until creamy and smooth. Season to taste. Add chopped parsley. Break pretzels into small pieces and add to soup just before serving.

Potato Soup

4 cups potatoes, diced
1 medium onion, chopped
3 tbsp. flour
1 tbsp. butter

1 qt. milk
1 egg, beaten
salt and pepper
parsley, chopped

Boil potatoes and onion in small amount of water until soft. Add milk, salt and pepper, and reheat. Brown flour in butter and blend slowly into the potato mixture. Add a little water to the beaten egg and stir into soup. Cook for a few minutes. Add chopped parsley and stir just before serving.

Miscellaneous Specialties

Fastnachts
(Raised Doughnuts)

For the sponge:
1 cake yeast
2 cups lukewarm water
4 scant cups all-purpose flour, sifted

For the dough:
1/2 cup shortening
3/8 cup sugar
1-1/2 tsp. salt
2 eggs, beaten

1/2 tsp. ground nutmeg
5 cups or more all-purpose
    flour, sifted
cooking oil

The night before frying doughnuts, break and soak yeast in lukewarm water for 20 minutes. Mix in flour and blend to a thick batter. Cover and let rise in warm place overnight until doubled.

In the morning, cream together shortening, sugar, and salt. Add to risen sponge with the beaten eggs and nutmeg. Stir in as much flour as mixture will readily take. Dough should be soft. Mix well. Cover and let rise until doubled. Turn onto a floured surface. Pat or roll until 1/3-inch thick. Cut out doughnuts with a cutter. Cover to prevent drying. Let rise until doubled. Fry in 375 degree oil until golden brown.

Pretzels

The word *pretzel* comes from the Latin word *pretiola*, which means "a small reward." Centuries ago in southern Europe, a pretzel was given by monks to children as a reward for learning prayers. The twist in the pretzel represents the crossed arms of a praying monk and the three spaces inside the pretzel shape represent the Trinity. Pretzels, both soft and hard, are a tradition among the Pennsylvania Germans.

Soft Pretzels

1 cup water (105-115 degrees)
1 pkg. active dry yeast
2-3/4 cups all-purpose flour, sifted

1/2 tsp. coarse salt
1 tbsp. sugar
5 tsp. baking soda

Combine water and yeast. When yeast is dissolved, add 1-1/2 cups flour, butter, salt and sugar. Beat 3 minutes. Stir in 1-1/4 cups flour. Knead until dough loses stickiness. Cover and let rise in a warm place until doubled. Punch down. Divide into 12 equal pieces. Roll pieces into 18-inch lengths, the thickness of a pencil. Loop into pretzel shape. Cover and let rise until almost doubled.

Add baking soda to 4 cups boiling water. With a slotted spoon, carefully lower pretzels into boiling solution for 1 minute. Remove to a greased cookie sheet and blot. Sprinkle with coarse salt. Bake in 475 degree oven for about 12 minutes.

Clear Candy Toys

An enduring tradition involves the preparation of "clear" candy toys. The term *clear* refers to the natural, amber color of the syrup. Red and green food dyes have become traditional additives. The children of early German settlers enjoyed clear toy candies as ornaments, toys, and a special treat to be eaten.

On Christmas Eve, children would set their plates on the kitchen table in hopes that "Krist-Kindel" would fill them with fruits, nuts, and clear toys. In later years, these same treats would be found in Christmas stockings.

Clear toy molds depicting animals, people, buildings, and scenes are still available. If stored properly in a dry place, clear toys can last for years.

Clear Candy Toys

molds, metal or appropriate plastic	cooking oil
2 cups granulated sugar	funnel, lightly oiled
2/3 cup light corn syrup	candy thermometer
1/2 cup water	

Blend sugar, corn syrup, and water in a saucepan. Place on high heat. Let syrup boil rapidly. Insert candy thermometer. When candy reaches 250 degrees, add coloring. *Do not stir.* Boiling action will distribute color evenly. Let temperature rise to 300 degrees. Quickly remove thermometer and remove pan from heat. Let bubbles subside. Pour quickly into funnel and deposit syrup into lightly oiled molds. Insert sticks if desired. Let cool slightly and unmold onto wax paper or a smooth surface. Candies can then be wrapped in plastic wrap or loosely stacked in an airtight container.

Apple Butter

10 lbs. apples	2 tbsp. ground allspice
6 qts. apple cider	2 tbsp. ground cloves
4 lbs. sugar	3 tbsp. ground cinnamon

Wash and quarter apples. Boil cider for 20 minutes. Add apples to cider and cook until very tender. Press through a sieve. Add sugar, allspice, cloves, and cinnamon to pulp. Cook on low heat to the consistency of soft paste, stirring constantly. Pour into crocks or glass jars. Refrigerate. Apple butter can be stored for months but cannot be frozen.

Red Beet Eggs

red beets (canned or jarred red beets can also be used)
eggs, hard-boiled
white vinegar, or cider vinegar
sugar

     Place whole red beets in water to cover. Boil until tender (1 to 3 hours). Discard cooking water. Skin and slice thinly. Place in a glass container with lid. Cover with vinegar. Let stand for several days. (If desired, add sugar to taste after a few days.) These steps are not necessary if using canned or jarred beets. Just add eggs.

     Hard-boil eggs and remove shells. Place eggs in container with beets and juice. Refrigerate. Eggs and beets will keep for several weeks.

Corn Fritters

2 eggs
2 tbsp. flour
2 cups grated fresh corn

1 tsp. salt
pepper

     Beat eggs. Add flour, salt, and pepper to taste. Add corn to dough. Drop small spoonfuls on greased griddle or fry pan. Cook over medium heat until lightly browned on both sides.

Part IV

Story Sources and
Selected Bibliography

Story Sources

Boyer, Walter E., et al. *Songs Along the Mahantongo*. Lancaster: Pennsylvania Dutch Folklore Center, 1951:
"Sleep, My Little Darling, Sleep" (melody), p. 31

Brendle, Thomas, and William Troxell. *Pennsylvania German Folktales, Legends, Once-Upon-a-Time Stories, Maxims, Sayings*, 1944:

(Brendle and Troxell dedicated their work to the Brothers Grimm because their purpose, like that of the Brothers Grimm, was to gather and preserve the stories of the Pennsylvania Germans while keeping the dialect intact. At the time, fewer and fewer were speaking the dialect. Fearing that the stories would become lost to future generations, the authors carefully recorded and translated the stories. For this volume, we have adapted the stories to make them more tellable for children.)

"Ascension Day," p. 82
"Ascension Thursday," p. 83
"The Bear and the Fox," p. 26
"The Best of Three," p. 94–95
"The Blind Man and the Giant," p. 24–25
"The Braucher," p. 143
"The Broom's the Thing," p. 145
"Counting Noses," p. 110–111.
"The Dance of the Nymphs," p. 131
"The Devil Cannot Do the Impossible," p. 148
"The Devil Does Not Recognize His Favorite Implement," p. 158–59
"Devil's Bit," p. 39
"Driving in the Peg," p. 138–39
"Eileschpiggel and the Cattle," p. 172–173.
"Eileschpiggel, the Farmhand," p. 162
"The Endless Story," p. 34
"The Eternal Hunter," p. 120–22
"Farming on Shares," p. 160–61
"The Father's Ghost," p. 133–34
"Geneova," p. 27–28.
"The Ghost of the Cornerstone," p. 122–23
"A Ghost Who Would Not Be Mocked," p. 130–31
"The Good Old Days," p. 146–47
"The Great Need," p. 31–33.
"The Horses That Couldn't Move," p. 97–98
"The Inquisitive Servant," p. 147–48

"Logic Is Logic," p. 163
"The Lost Plant," p. 42
"Lousewort," p. 41
"Peeling the Apple," p. 93–94
"Pimpernell," p. 44
"The Plant with the Blood Spots," p. 41
"The Pot of Gold," p. 126
"The Princess That Would Not Laugh," p. 30–31
"The Rabbit and the Bear," p. 34–36
"The Sewing Contest," p. 154–55
"The Speaking Horses," p. 79
"Speedwell," p. 43–44
"The Spirit of the Faithful Son," p. 132–33
"Swamp Pink," p. 40
"The Swimming Contest," p. 155
"The Witches Are Riding," p. 145–46

Crisp, Marty. "Hex, It's Art." *Sunday News*, August 15, 1993:
"The Story of the Distelfink" (adaptation title)

Frey, Dorothy (Lancaster County Pennsylvania storyteller):
"Big John and the Devil" (adaptation title)
"Pennsylvania Dutchmen Always Give Testimony" (adaptation title)

Frey, Howard C. "Conestoga Wagoners." *Pennsylvania Songs and Legends.*
Philadelphia: University of Pennsylvania Press, 1949:
"The Unusual Apple," p. 247
"The Well-Trained Horses," p. 247
"The Wild March Wind," p. 247

Frey, J. William, ed. "Schnitzelbank." *The Pennsylvania Dutchman* 1, no.
5 (June 1949):
"Schnitzelbank" (melody), p. 7

Miller, Grace (Lancaster County, Pennsylvania storyteller):
"The Big Sinkhole" (adaptation title)

Mumau, John R. "Mennonite Folklore." *Pennsylvania Folklife* 11, no. 1
(spring 1960):
"ABC," p. 39
"Counting Out Rhyme," p. 39
"The Dishonest Milkman," p. 38
"I Will Show You," p. 39
"Incantation to Call for Rain," p. 38
"Little Barbara," p. 39
"Little Mare," p. 39

"Needle and Thread Riddle," p. 39
"A Nonsense Rhyme," p. 38

Shoemaker, Alfred L. "Pennsylvania German Rhymes and Jingles." *The Pennsylvania Dutchman* 1, no. 1 (May 1949):
"Backa, Backa, Kucha," p. 2
"This One Is the Thumb," p. 2

Shoemaker, Alfred L. "Pennsylvania German Rhymes and Jingles." *The Pennsylvania Dutchman* 1, no. 2 (May 1949):
"Giddap! Giddap! Little Horsey," p. 2
"Heeli, Heeli, Hinkel Dreck," p. 2
"Seasonal Rhyme," p. 2

Shoemaker, Alfred L. "Pennsylvania German Rhymes and Jingles." *The Pennsylvania Dutchman* 1, no. 9 (June 1949):
"One Gets Wet When It Rains," p. 2

Shoemaker, Alfred L. "Pennsylvania German Rhymes and Jingles." *The Pennsylvania Dutchman* 2, no. 3 (May 1950):
"Fish Swim in Fog," p. 2

Shoemaker, Alfred L. *Traditional Rhymes and Jingles of the Pennsylvania Dutch*, 1951:
"The Almanac Rhyme," p. 7
"Here There Sits a Mouse," p. 5
"Schlofe, Bubbely, Schlofe," p. 5

Smith, Elmer. *Pennsylvania Dutch Folklore*, 1990:
"A Master Farmer" (adaptation title), from "A Expert Farmer," p. 16
"The Big Lehigh Pig," p. 17
"Early to Rise," p. 17

Books

Adams, Charles J., III. *Pennsylvania Dutch Country Ghost Legends and Lore.* Reading, PA: Exeter House Book, 1994.

Ammon, Richard. *Growing Up Amish.* New York: Atheneum, 1989.

Aurand, A. Monroe, Jr. *Quaint Idioms and Expressions of the Pennsylvania Germans.* Lancaster, PA: Aurand Press.

Barrick, Mae E., ed. *German-American Folklore.* Little Rock, AR: August House, 1987.

Beam, C. Richard. *Abridged Pennsylvania German Dictionary.* Millersville, PA: Center for Pennsylvania German Studies, Millersville University, 1993.

———. *Revised Pennsylvania German Dictionary: English to Pennsylvania Dutch.* Lancaster, PA: Brookshire, 1994.

Boyer, Walter E., Alvert F. Buffington, and Don Yoder. *Songs Along the Mahantongo Valley.* Lancaster, PA: Pennsylvania Dutch Folklore Center, 1951.

Butler, Jon. *The Huguenots in America.* Cambridge, MA: Harvard University Press, 1983.

Byler, Emma. *Plain and Happy Living: Amish Recipes and Remedies.* Cleveland, OH: Goosefoot Acres Press, 1991.

Costabel, Eva Deutsch. *The Pennsylvania Dutch: Craftsmen and Farmers.* New York: Atheneum, 1986.

Denlinger, A. Martha. *Real People: Amish and Mennonites in Lancaster County*, 4th ed. Scottdale, PA: Herald Press, 1993.

Faill, Carol E., et al. *Fraktur: A Selective Guide to the Franklin and Marshall Fraktur Collection.* Lancaster, PA: Franklin and Marshall College, 1987.

Gladfelter, Charles. *The Pennsylvania Germans: A Brief Account of Their Influence on Pennsylvania.* Harrisburg, PA: Pennsylvania Historical Society, 1990.

Good, Phyllis Pellman, and Daughter. *Amish Cooking for Kids.* Intercourse, PA: Good Books, 1995.

Good, Phyllis Pellman, and Louise Stoltzfus. *The Central Market Cookbook.* Intercourse, PA: Good Books, 1989.

Hark, Ann. *Blue Hills and Shoo-Fly Pie.* Philadelphia: J. B. Lippincott, 1952.

———. *Hex Marks the Spot.* Philadelphia: J. B. Lippincott, 1938.

Heiberger, Rose. *Buggy Seat, Bare Feet.* Gordonville, PA: Print Shop, 1995.

Herrera, J. E. *Funny Stories: Pennsylvania Dutch Wit and Humor.* Gettysburg, PA: Dutchcraft, 1966.

Horning, Paul B. *Folk Tales and Such Like.* Community Historians Annual, no. 15, Schaff Library. Lancaster, PA: Lancaster Theological Seminary, 1976.

———. *Thirteen Tramps.* Community Historians Annual, no. 14, Schaff Library. Lancaster, PA: Lancaster Theological Seminary, 1975.

Hostetler, John A., ed. *Amish Roots.* Baltimore, MD: Johns Hopkins University Press, 1992.

Jordan, Mildred. *The Shoo-Fly Pie.* New York: Alfred A. Knopf, 1944.

Kauffman, Henry J. *Pennsylvania Dutch American Folk Art.* Elverson, PA: Olde Springfield Shoppe, 1993.

Klee, Frederic. *The Pennsylvania Dutch.* New York: Macmillan, 1950.

Knisely, Kim Gehman. *A Is for Amish.* Lititz, PA: Knisely Stoltzfus Books, 1993.

Korson, George, ed. *Pennsylvania Songs and Legends.* Philadelphia: University of Pennsylvania Press, 1949.

Leach, MacEdward, and Henry Glassie. *A Guide for Collectors of Oral Traditions and Folk Culture Material in Pennsylvania.* Harrisburg, PA: Commonwealth of Pennsylvania, Pennsylvania Historical and Museum Commission, 1968.

Lund, Adrienne. *The Amish Way: Cookbook and Home Remedies.* Chagrin Falls, OH: Jupiter Press, 1994.

Milhous, Katherine. *The Egg Tree.* New York: Aladdin Books, 1978.

Mitchell, Edwin Valentine. *It's an Old Pennsylvania Custom.* New York: Bonanza Books, 1947.

Pellman, Rachel, and Kenneth Pellman. *A Treasury of Amish Quilts.* Intercourse, PA: Good Books, 1992.

Reist, Arthur L. *Conestoga Wagon—Masterpiece of the Blacksmith.* Lancaster, PA: Forry and Hacker, 1975.

Scott, Stephen. *Why Do They Dress That Way?* Intercourse, PA: Good Books, 1986.

Shoemaker, Alfred L. *Traditional Rhymes and Jingles of the Pennsylvania Dutch.* Lancaster, PA: Pennsylvania Dutch Folklore Center, circa 1948-1950.

Smith, Elmer L., ed. *Pennsylvania Dutch Folklore.* Lebanon, PA: Applied Arts, 1990.

Weaver, William Woys. *Sauerkraut Yankees: Pennsylvania German Foods and Foodways.* Philadelphia: University of Pennsylvania Press, 1983.

Wentz, Richard, ed. *Pennsylvania Dutch: Folk Spirituality.* Mahwah, NJ: Paulist Press, 1993.

Wood, Ralph, ed. *The Pennsylvania Germans.* Princeton, NJ: Princeton University Press, 1942.

Yoder, Don. *Discovering American Folklife: Studies in Ethnic, Religious and Regional Culture.* Ann Arbor, MI: IMI Research Press, 1990.

Articles

Drachman, Albert I. "Tracking the Elusive Distelfink." *The Dutchman* 6, no. 5 (1955): 28–35.

Kauffman, Henry J. "Literature on Log Literature—A Survey." *The Dutchman* 7, no. 2 (1955): 30–34.

Mummaw, John R. "Mennonite Folklore." *Pennsylvania Folklife* 11, no. 1 (1960): 38–40.

Newell, William M. "Schuylkill Folktales." *Pennsylvania Folklife* 9, no. 3 (1958): 18–19.

Robacker, Earl F. "Basketry, a Pennsylvania Dutch Art." *The Dutchman* 7, no. 2 (1955): 2–6.

———. "Cutting Up for Fancy." *Pennsylvania Folklife* 10, no. 2 (1959): 2–10.

———. "Pennsylvania Gaudyware." *The Dutchman* 7, no. 4 (1956): 2–7.

———. "The Peacock in Pennsylvania." *Pennsylvania Folklife* 11, no. 1 (1960): 10–16.

Shoemaker, Alfred L. "Rhymes and Jingles." *The Dutchman* 1, no. 1 (1949): 2.

———. *The Dutchman* 1, no. 2 (1949): 2.

———. *The Dutchman* 1, no. 9 (1949): 2.

Smith, Linda Joan. "Sunday Best." *Country Home*, April 1993, 58–64.

About the Authors

Audrey Burie Kirchner

Audrey is Professor of Education (Elementary and Early Childhood) at Millersville University in Millersville, Pennsylvania. *In Days Gone By* is her fourth book. Her previous works include *Reading with A Smile, Basic Beginnings,* and *Multicultural Explorations.* She is a member of the International Reading Association, National Council of Teachers of English, National Association for the Education of Young Children, and the Association for Childhood Education International. She has worked with children from the preschool level through the elementary years.

Margaret R. Tassia

Margaret is Professor of Education in the Elementary and Early Childhood Education department at Millersville University in Millersville, Pennsylvania. She is a member of the Pennsylvania School Librarians Association and was the recipient of the Outstanding Contributor to School Libraries Award. She is active in the American Library Association, American Association of School Librarians. *In Days Gone By* is her second book; she previously co-authored *Games for Information Skills* with Audrey Kirchner.